Bridging Foo

~ An Introduction to gluten, dairy and yeast free eating ~

First published in Australia 2011 by:
Bridging Foods
31 Bourke St - Yokine - Perth - Australia 6060
www.bridgingfoods.com.au

National Library of Australian Cataloguing-in-Publication entry:
Authors: Sjardin, Nicole and Scott, Sally - Bridging Foods

1st Edition
ISBN 978-0-646-52171-8

Editors: Gabriele Conrad & Natalie Benhayon

Design and typesetting by Désirée Delaloye – www.design-arts.com.au

Front cover and all other photography by Lee Green

Colour reproduction by Flawless Imaging, Clayton Lloyd – www.flawlessimaging.com

Taste testers: Jacob Levin, Madeline Lynch, Samuel Levin

Printed and bound in China by Everbest Printing Co LTD EVERBEST

Visit the Bridging Foods website www.bridgingfoods.com.au
or send us an email via info@bridgingfoods.com.au

The energetic truths and principles in this book
are based on the work and teachings
of Serge Benhayon, www.universalmedicine.com.au

The authors acknowledge his work as the source of inspiration and,
the permissible copyright material.

A special thank you to Natalie Benhayon.

We would like to acknowledge and thank everyone
who has given us permission to share their recipes.

The recipes were chosen because of the energetic imprint,
inspiring us to BE in our kitchens and to cook with love.

Content

SECTION ONE

AN INTRODUCTION TO GLUTEN, DAIRY AND YEAST FREE EATING

BRIDGING FOODS	2
GLUTEN FREE FLOURS	8
FOOD LIST	10
TIPS	14

SECTION TWO

BRIDGING FOODS

BREAKFAST	19
SNACKS	37
DIPS	59
SALADS	71
SOUPS	81
MAINS	93
ACCOMPANIMENTS	123
STOCKS, SAUCES & DRESSINGS	133
BISCUITS & MUFFINS	145
DESSERTS	157

Section 1

~ An Introduction to gluten, dairy and yeast free eating ~

BRIDGING FOODS

GLUTEN FREE FLOURS

FOOD LIST

TIPS

BRIDGING FOODS
– AN INTRODUCTION TO GLUTEN, DAIRY AND YEAST FREE EATING

"If everything is energy, therefore, everything is because of energy."
~ Serge Benhayon[1]

If we consider the above quote as a possibility, how would this have an impact on how we buy, prepare, cook and eat food? If we choose to explore the above, we can begin to notice that different foods have an effect on our bodies that precedes those induced by the nutrients or chemicals of any particular food item. Do we choose to eat by listening to what our body shows us as being supportive or not supportive, or by what other people tell us is 'good' and 'healthy'? Have we always eaten by what others say our body needs, or could we let our own bodies guide us to what we truly need for ourselves? If we explore this possibility, we can start to become more aware of our eating habits and/or cravings and take a step back to look at what is motivating us when we buy, prepare and eat certain foods.

Here are familiar scenarios that you may have experienced around your food choices:

Have you ever been emotional because of an event that has happened and then chosen food that you think will make you feel better or comfort you in some way? *For example:* A relationship break-up followed by eating a whole tub of ice cream, a whole packet of chocolate biscuits or a block of chocolate – does this actually help the emotional experience or does it distract you from how you are really feeling?

What about the child that is fed too much sugar, sweet drinks, lollies and ice cream which then impacts on their energy levels? The child goes hyperactive for a while, then their energy drops and they may be moody and tired which has them asking for more of the sugary foods.

A family Christmas where everyone eats too much food and drinks too much alcohol and then the afternoon is spent feeling uncomfortable or you fall asleep.

Choosing to drink something containing caffeine because you feel tired and need a quick energy fix, but that 'quick fix' is not supporting your body to feel energised long-term.

Have you ever used a diet regime, something that someone else has prescribed or suggested because you want your body to look a certain way? Maybe there was an event you wanted to lose weight for, a graduation or party, a wedding or to see someone you hadn't seen in a long time. Have you found that this weight loss has been hard to maintain or not at all sustainable?

These are everyday examples of how we are with food and diet – could the reason why we are choosing to eat or diet in a certain way as well as the ingredients in the food that we eat, also be a factor that contributes to the imbalances in our bodies?

Your food choices may be influenced by many factors:

– your emotional state

– your family and friends

– your energy levels, and

– how you feel about yourself and what you do for yourself.

You may lovingly prepare a meal and then allow yourself time to sit down and enjoy this meal without any distractions around you. This may include not eating on the run, turning off the television, not doing other things while you eat, or choosing not to overeat to comfort or stimulate yourself. These are supportive and loving choices that could be made in relation to food.

> ***"Feel what to eat ~ not eat what you feel."***
>
> ~ Miranda Benhayon[2]

Over time we have found that certain foods affect how our bodies feel. Some of these are listed below:

GLUTEN

Gluten is a protein found in grains: wheat, rye, oats, barley, spelt and triticale. The word GLUTEN is derived from the Latin word for 'glue'. Is this a coincidence? We don't think so. In the body, gluten can interfere with the small hair like structures that line the entire digestive tract. Gluten literally flattens these structures (like glue!) inhibiting further breakdown of food and the absorption of nutrients. This gives rise to a whole host of digestive complaints, the most common being bloating and gas. Gluten can also make the body feel heavy or sleepy after you eat it, so it is a good idea to watch out for these signs and anything else your body may exhibit that is unique to you. Start to be aware of any signals your body may be using to get your attention. Our bodies constantly talk to us, but do we listen?

WHEAT

Wheat is a grain that contains gluten and thus is also difficult for the body to digest. Most store bought products are based on wheat or wheat flour. It is in our breakfast cereals, our bread, crackers, cakes, pastries, pasta, confectionary, savoury snack items … it's everywhere. It has been suggested that due to the constant daily overexposure to this grain, many of the population have become sensitive to it. Another issue with wheat and wheat flour is that it turns to simple sugars very quickly, because it has been so highly processed. This dramatically spikes the blood sugar levels, feeding the yeast/ bacteria/fungi in the digestive tract (causing all sorts of digestive upsets) and affecting mood, concentration and energy levels.

CARBOHYDRATES

They are a food that gives the body a quick fix because it converts into simple sugars, which give the body a false energy boost and make it feel racy. The carbohydrates, which cause a sudden spike in blood sugar levels, include: bread, toast, crackers, grains, most breakfast cereals, rice, potato, pasta and tropical fruits. Other carbohydrates such as fruit (pears, apples, berries etc) and vegetables do not turn to simple sugars as readily. Constant daily spiking of blood sugar levels puts a huge demand on the pancreas. Over time the pancreas gets tired and bothered and cannot produce enough hormones to appropriately control the blood sugar levels. The people affected then experience health issues and need medication to support the job the pancreas naturally does. Is it possible that our Standard Australian Diet (S.A.D) being cereal for breakfast, a sandwich for lunch and pasta plus meat for dinner, an unnaturally high consumption of carbohydrates, is contributing to the demise of our health and vitality?

YEAST

Yeasted products such as bread, crackers, most stock cubes/powders, Vegemite, beer etc feed the yeasts naturally found in our digestive tract. All too often and from a very early age, because of our overconsumption of products containing yeast and sugar, we develop a yeast overgrowth. Sugar feeds the yeasts/bacteria/fungi in the digestive system and makes them grow and proliferate. This overgrowth gives rise to many health concerns, including digestive issues (gas, bloating, thrush), lowered immunity, fungal skin problems (such as athlete's foot, tinea etc), mood fluctuations, chronic tiredness and much, much more! Often we see that people crave these yeasted foods because the yeast microbes produce "aldehydes", which basically act like alcohol in the body. This in turn becomes very addictive and is the reason why people want more of the same, and it turns into a repetitious harmful cycle.

DAIRY

There are hundreds of scientific studies done on cow's milk all over the world and its deleterious effects in the human body. Studies have linked milk to infantile constipation, colic, to adolescent acne, to adult infertility, cardiovascular issues, prostate cancer and more.

There is a lot of misinformation about dairy and the calcium it provides. *For example:*

FOOD ITEM	CALCIUM ABSORBED PER 100 CALORIES
Whole Milk	61
Low Fat Yoghurt with fruit	45
Choy Sum	860
Bok Choy	425
Wakame (sea vegetable)	113
Chinese Spinach	110

A system to assess the quality of food sources of calcium, Titchenal, Joannie Dobbs. Human Nutrition, Food and Animal Sciences, University of Hawaii.

It is clear from this table that there are many more bio-available sources of calcium other than milk and milk products. If we were to ask you "where do cows get the calcium they put into their milk?" one would say, "ahhh … from the grass they eat." This is correct. Cow's milk is PERFECT for baby calves. They have four stomachs to digest it. Us humans, have only one stomach. We were never designed to drink another animal's milk.

The study above shows that green leafy vegetables are top quality sources of calcium. Other calcium rich foods include almonds, sesame seeds (black and white), tofu, kale, natural mineral waters and Japanese sea vegetables. These food sources come flawlessly designed with co-nutrients to support calcium absorption without the negative attributes of dairy products. It is very common for dairy products to contribute to irritable bowel syndrome, colic-like abdominal pain and diarrhoea. It has also been shown that, when people who are prone to respiratory tract mucus including sinus problems and asthma eliminate dairy products from their diet, their symptoms improve. You might like to experiment on yourself and eliminate dairy products for 4 - 6 weeks from your diet and see how you feel.

SUGAR

Sugar artificially boosts the energy in the body and can make you feel racy. Sugar consumption has grown enormously since the industrial revolution. Sugar is in most commercial food products such as peanut butter, tomato sauce, breakfast cereals, snack bars and more. There are over 65 different names for sugar which the food industry uses in their ingredients lists. All too often sugar is in the top 3 ingredients. Please read the ingredients labels very carefully. Apart from spiking blood sugar levels, sugar feeds the yeasts and bacteria in the digestive tract causing many imbalances in the gut flora. Sugar has also been shown to have damaging effects on the immune system. To break down one molecule of sugar, you need around 56 molecules of magnesium. Is it any wonder we have a widespread magnesium deficiency in our population?

Note: the above list and the descriptions of the true activity that these foods have in our body have been provided by "The Healing Ingredient" founded by Nina Stabey (Naturopath/Nutritionist). It is knowledge known to many, and here provided for you to have a greater understanding of what these foods are doing in your physical body so you can make a healthier and informed decision of what you will or will not put into it. With the above knowledge, we can start to be more aware and then be honest about what certain foods are doing to us and how they make us feel.

It is important to note that this book is NOT A DIET GUIDE. It is presenting the possibility for you to not just use a recipe but to have a sense of your body and how food makes you feel. Preparing food and eating is a loving and nourishing daily task, and making changes need not be tasteless and tedious. The recipes in this book are gluten, dairy and yeast free and low in sugar. This is a collection of recipes that we have found useful as we ourselves are learning to be more aware of how certain foods affect the way our body feels, and how supportive or not the meals feel to our body throughout the day. We are presenting this book as a bridge to learning that eating and cooking gluten, dairy and yeast free can be easy, tasty and full of love and joy.

Bridging Foods is a book that gives you an opportunity to consider how food makes you feel. It asks you to not just use the recipes but to consider that there is a lot more going on for us and our relationship with food. In truth, when you feel what to cook, the recipe would change every time you use it, based on how you are feeling. Feel into every recipe and ingredient and determine whether it is right for you or not. Every ingredient that you use and the way you are feeling whilst you cook affect the end result, and by adding this awareness as an ingredient to the recipes, food takes on a whole new flavour.

En-joy ...

GLUTEN FREE FLOURS

Amaranth flour –
Has a high percentage of protein and fibre.

Arrowroot flour (tapioca) –
Good for thickening fruit sauces. Has no real flavour of its own.

Buckwheat flour –
Just to clear things up: it has nothing to do with wheat. It has a distinct nutty flavour and is often used to make pancakes.

Channa flour (besan or chickpea flour) –
It is commonly used in indian cooking as a thickener and in breads and pancakes.

Chestnut flour –
A little sweet, traditionally used in italian desserts.

Coconut flour –
Low in carbohydrates. A very delicate coconut flavour, a very soft flour and ideal for cakes. It holds the moisture, allowing for a light cake.

Cornmeal (polenta) –
It can come in fine and course textures. It can be used as a coating and is versatile in absorbing flavours in sweet and savoury bakes.

Masa, Masa Harina or Mesca flour –
Comes from white, yellow or blue corn treated with lime. Used for home-made tortillas and corn bread.

Maize (cornflour) –

Is popular in asian cooking and gives sauces a clear smooth thickness.
It is useful when texture is needed, for example in shortbread. When choosing cornflour, make sure it is labelled gf.

Pea flour –

Has a coarse texture and strong flavour. Good for a coating mixture for batters and fritters. Similar to chickpea flour.

Quinoa flour –

Helps retain moisture in baked goods.

Soy flour –

Has a creamy yellow colour.

Tapioca flour –

From the dried starch of the cassava root, thickens when heated with water.

Urid flour –

Commonly used in indian cooking to make flat breads, chapattis and pappadoms. It is a very fine flour made from grinding urid dhal.

FOOD LIST

This list provides gluten and dairy free products that are useful to have in your pantry.

Over time your pantry takes on a feel that is in tune with your energetic state of being and awareness.

... IN THE PANTRY

- **Agar agar powder**
- **Agave syrup or nectar** – a natural unrefined sweetener from the agave plant.
- **Almond meal**
- **Baked beans** – check ingredients and avoid buying brands with stabilisers and thickeners.
- **Baking powder** – gluten and aluminium free.
- **Baking mix** – a mixture of gf flours ready to use for a variety of cooking options, or make your own mix. Try soy, potato or tapioca flours.
- **Bread** – gf, df.
- **Coconut milk and cream** – most coconut milks and creams contain mainly water with added thickeners or stabilisers. Try to find one that is 100% coconut.
- **Coconut oil** – solid at room temperature, great for all types of cooking. Pressed (filtered through clay) it has less of a coconut flavour.
- **Cornflour** – check that the brand is gf.
- **Corn chips** – gf.
- **Cornflakes** – normal cornflakes are made from wheat. In the health food aisle of your supermarket you will find gf cornflakes. These can be used as cereals and for baking.

- **Corn thins** – check ingredients as not all are gf, df.
- **Crumbs** – gf breadcrumbs or rice crumbs.
- **Curry powder**
- **Dried fruits and nuts**
- **Felafel mix** – gf, df.
- **Fish sauce** – check that it is gf as some contain thickeners.
- **Flour** – plain and self-raising, gf.
- **Fruit concentrate** (apple or pear).
- **Gravy mix** – gf, df.
- **Honey** – raw unprocessed honey.
- **Herbs and spices** – rather than packet stocks and/or sauces.
- **LSA** – a meal of ground linseeds, sunflower seeds and almonds.
- **Pure maple syrup**
- **Pasta** – gf or try the rice and corn substitutes.
- **Pizza base** – gf, df.
- **Polenta**
- **Popcorn**
- **Quinoa** – flakes and/or grain, you can buy white, red or black quinoa.
- **Rice crackers** – check ingredients as not all are gf, df.
- **Rice paper or sheets**
- **Rice noodles**
- **Sea salt** – make sure it is of good quality and not iodised.
- **Sea vegetables** – nutrient packed and add great flavour to a variety of dishes.
  Nori seaweed sheets – use for sushi, as a wrap or on salads.

Arame – great addition to salads and stir fries.

Kombu – a great base for soups, stews and stocks, contains glutamic acid which really brings out the flavour in your cooking.

Wakame – mild in flavour, can also be used in salads and soups.

- *Tamari* – wf, as a substitute for soya sauce.

- *Tamarind pulp concentrate* – made from tamarind pulp and water, it has a sour flavour.

- *Ume Su (umeboshi vinegar)* – unfermented and very salty juice from umeboshi plums, can be used in all types of cooking and for dressings or dips.

- *Vermicelli noodles* – made from beans.

- *Verjuice* – made from the unfermented juice of young fruit, usually grapes. Verjuice is like vinegar but minus the bite. Its acid content is around half that of vinegar. Substitute it for vinegar in mayonnaise and vinaigrette, use it to deglaze, or add it to a casserole to sharpen it up a bit. Look for it in the vinegar section of your supermarket.

- *Wasabi* – some preparations contain a dairy based ingredient.

- *White corn tortillas* – found in the bread or taco section of supermarkets.

- *Xanthan gum or guar gum* – used in gluten free baking to help create structure.

NOTES

TIPS

- Stop and look at the energy you are in when you buy, prepare and eat certain foods.

- Preparing and eating food can be a loving and a nourishing thing to do.

- The food you cook is for you, so be open to changing the recipe so it feels right for you.

- Read labels on food packaging, continue to check labels, even those you think you are sure of, as information can change.

- Observe how your body feels when you eat certain foods.

- Be aware of the glamour in diets. Most importantly, feel into products and food. Just because it is gf, wf and df does not mean it is the right food choice for you.

- When stirring any food, use a figure eight movement and/or stir anti-clockwise.

- Visit 'Coeliac World Wide' on the internet, www.coeliacworldwide.com.au as they have a list of resources for gluten intolerance. As they say on their website: "you are what you absorb."

- Start walking down the health food aisle in your supermarket to find wheat, dairy and gluten free alternatives.

- If possible, go to different supermarkets to look at their health food section as different supermarkets stock different products.

- Talk to your local butcher about ordering in gluten free meat products if they do not already stock a gluten free range of ham, bacon and sausages.

- It may take some time, but if you look around you may find a bakery that does gf, df and sugar free breads. Alternatively, ask your supermarket or health food shop to assist you, and they may be able to order it in for you on a regular basis.

- When baking, try different combinations of gf flours rather than always using the same one.

- Continue to use your favourite recipes and substitute the ingredients for the gf, df and sf alternatives you have found.

- When cooking with gf flours, they will generally absorb more liquid than wheat flour, so you may need to experiment with recipes and the amount of wet ingredients that you need.

- When baking, be mindful that cooking with gluten free flours is something that takes practice – oven temperature is important, ring tins work well as you don't end up with a soggy middle and experiment with different combinations of gf flours.
  Try substituting nut meal for flour.

- Slowly begin to change the products sitting in your pantry, fridge and freezer and do not become overwhelmed or stressed about your food choices.

- To support yourself in your decision to be gf, df and sf, carry snack foods with you that lovingly support this choice.

- There are more and more products available for gf, df and sf cooking. So continue to look out for new products.

- Shout yourself at least one cookbook that supports and inspires your new eating choices.

- When spending time cooking, go with what feels right for you and be playful.

Section 2

Breakfast

Snacks

Dips

Salads

Soups

Mains

Accompaniments

Stocks, Sauces & Dressings

Biscuits & Muffins

Desserts

~ Breakfast ~

OBSERVATIONS

Be aware that some breakfast cereals like cornflakes and rice bubbles can contain gluten.

Look in the health food aisle of your supermarket/s for breakfast cereals that are gf, wf.

If cereals are labelled wf they are not necessarily gf.

Oats – oats do not contain gluten. Oats do however interact with our bodies in the same way gluten does and energetically, our bodies are affected.

Fruit & Nut Loaf | Rhubarb & Pear Compote with Nut Cream | Sausage Roast

CLASSIC CHOPPED FRUIT & NUTS

serves 1

Ingredients

half an apple – chopped

half a pear – chopped

1/2 cup (80g) fresh pineapple – chopped

4 strawberries – chopped

1/4 cup (40g) blueberries

1 tablespoon fresh mint – chopped

1 tablespoon LSA (ground linseed, sunflower seeds and almonds)

1/3 cup (44g) chopped nuts
(pecans, walnuts, hazelnuts, macadamias)

Method

Place all the fruit in a bowl and mix well.

Sprinkle the LSA and chopped nuts over the top.

INSPIRATION

Serve with Nut Cream (see page 21).

NUT CREAM

Ingredients

1 cup (125g) nuts –
cashews, almonds, macadamias

1 1/2 cups (375ml) liquid – water,
gf soymilk, coconut cream or df, gf milk

optional sweetener – banana,mango cheek,
raw unprocessed honey or
pure maple syrup

1 teaspoon vanilla essence

1 teaspoon cinnamon

Method

Place all ingredients in a blender and mix until thick and creamy.

Choose one of the optional sweeteners.

Serve with chopped fresh fruit or the Rhubarb & Pear Compote (see page 22).

RHUBARB & PEAR COMPOTE

serves 4

Ingredients

1 bunch (x6 stalks) rhubarb – chopped

4 bosc pears (brown) – decored and sliced

juice from 1/2 to 1 orange

zest from 1 orange

1 cinnamon stick – broken up

2-3 tablespoons pure maple syrup

2 cloves

Method

Pre-heat oven to 180C.

Place all ingredients in an ovenproof dish.

Put in the oven uncovered for 45 minutes.

Check the compote and give it a stir.

Remove cinnamon and cloves from compote.

If needed, leave for a further 15 minutes before serving.

INSPIRATION

Serve with Nut Cream (see page 21).

BREAKFAST QUINOA (WITH APPLE & BLUEBERRIES)

serves 2

Ingredients

1 cup (185g) red quinoa

2 cups (500ml) water

1 teaspoon cinnamon

1 apple – sliced

1/2 cup (80g) blueberries

almond milk

Method

Add red quinoa and water to a small saucepan and bring to the boil.

Add the cinnamon.

After a few minutes, add the apple and give it a good stir.

Cook until liquid has been absorbed.

Before serving, stir through the blueberries and/or strawberries.

Serve with almond milk.

INSPIRATION

A rice cooker can also be used to cook red quinoa using the same ratio of 1 cup (160g) red quinoa to 2 cups (500ml) liquid.

Add red quinoa to rice cooker with water, cinnamon and apple and leave to cook. When serving, stir through blueberries and almond milk.

Add red quinoa to rice cooker with equal quantities of gf soy or coconut milk and water, add freshly grated ginger and orange zest and leave to cook.

ALMOND & CHICKPEA BREAKFAST PANCAKE

serves 4

Ingredients

3/4 cup (110g) almond meal

3/4 cup (110g) chickpea flour (besan)

1 free range egg – lightly whisked

1 cup (250ml) gf soy or almond milk

vanilla extract (optional)

olive oil

Method

Combine almond meal, chickpea flour, egg and milk in a small bowl and whisk until smooth.

Heat oil in a 18cm frying pan over medium heat.

Pour a ladle of batter, approximately 1/4 cup, into the frying pan.

Cook until bubbles appear evenly on the surface and pancakes are golden underneath.

Turn and cook for a further 1-2 minutes or until golden brown and cooked through.

Remove from heat.

Serve immediately.

INSPIRATION

Serve with cooked gf bacon, a fried egg and drizzle over some chilli oil.

Spread with hummus (see page 62), avocado and sea salt and pepper.

Serve topped with fresh banana and passionfruit.

Serve with chopped strawberries and pure maple syrup.

Serve with sugar free fruit spread.

CREPES

makes 12

Ingredients

2 cups (280g) gf flour

2 free range eggs plus 1 egg yolk

2 cups (250ml) df, gf milk

1/3 cup (85ml) water

oil for cooking

absorbent towel

Method

Place flour in a bowl.

Add eggs and egg yolk.

Add liquid, mixing until smooth.

Transfer mixture into a jug.

Heat olive oil in a frying pan (choose the frying pan according to the size of crepes desired).

Wipe excess oil from the pan with absorbent towel.

Pour batter into frying pan, the amount depends on the size and thickness of your crepes.

As you cook your crepes, simply rub the absorbent towel, soaked with oil, over the frying pan in between crepes.

Add more oil in between crepes if needed.

To keep crepes warm and moist, place cooked crepes on a plate which sits as a lid on top of a saucepan with simmering water.

INSPIRATION

You can play with the liquid amount in this recipe to also create pancakes or pikelets.

BANANA & EGG PANCAKE

makes 12

Ingredients

2 bananas

6 free range eggs

1 teaspoon vanilla extract

1 teaspoon cinnamon

Method

Place ingredients in a blender and blend until smooth.

Pour mixture into a warm frying pan and cook until well done before flipping the pancake over.

FRUIT & NUT LOAF

Ingredients

1 packet gf bread mix

3/4 cup (120g) dried fruit and or nuts – chopped

1 teaspoon cinnamon

Method

Pre-heat oven to 190C.

Follow instructions on packet to make bread.

Add fruit and nuts and cinnamon.

Pour into greased loaf tin and let rise to surface.

Place into oven and cook as instructed on the packet.

Remove when golden brown.

Leave in the tin for 5 minutes to cool slightly and then turn it out on a wire rack.

Cut into thick slices, and serve fresh or toasted.

CORN FRITTERS (WITH SALMON & ROCKET)

makes 10

Ingredients

2 1/4 cups (200g) corn kernels

2 tablespoons gf plain flour

1 free range egg – separated

df, gf milk (enough to make a smooth batter)

1/4 diced red capsicum (optional)

pepper

1 tablespoon fresh parsley – chopped

olive oil for frying

Method

Mash half the corn in a bowl.

Combine with flour, egg yolk, milk and pepper to form a thick batter.

Stir in all the corn and parsley (add diced capsicum if using it).

Whisk the egg white till soft peaks form, and gently fold into the batter (careful to keep the air bubbles in the mixture).

Heat the oil in a large frying pan.

Add 1 tablespoon of the mixture for each fritter, wait until it turns brown at the edges, turn carefully and cook for a short time on the other side.

INSPIRATION

Serve with a layer of gf bacon or smoked salmon, a layer of fresh rocket, and mashed avocado mixed with chilli sauce.

FRITTATA WITH TUNA, SPROUTS & TOMATO

serves 2

Ingredients

2 free range eggs – beaten

1/4 cup (63ml) df, gf milk

95g tin tuna – drained

1 tomato – sliced

handful sunflower sprouts

sea salt and pepper

1 teaspoon oil

Method

Beat the eggs and milk in a bowl until well combined and fluffy.

Add sea salt and pepper.

Heat oil in a large frying pan.

Pour the egg and milk mixture into the pan and cook over low heat.

Gently place tomato slices around the frittata and then cover with the drained tuna, cook for 5 minutes.

Sprinkle sprouts onto the frittata.

Place frittata under the grill for 5 minutes to cook the top.

Or place a dinner plate over the frying pan, invert turning frittata out onto the plate, flipping it over and gently sliding it back into the pan to cook the other side.
Cook for 3-5 minutes more.

Serve.

INSPIRATION

Use chopped gf ham, english spinach and capsicum as an alternative filling.

HOMEMADE BAKED BEANS

serves 6

Ingredients

1 handful each marjoram, thyme and oregano – roughly chopped

8 rashers gf bacon or 200g gf pancetta – chopped into cubes

3 shallots (french onion) – finely chopped

4 cloves garlic – finely chopped

2 sticks celery – finely cubed

1 carrot – finely cubed

2 small zucchini – finely cubed

1 leek – finely sliced

400g tin tomatoes

85g tomato paste

100ml extra virgin olive oil

1/2 chilli – finely chopped (add to taste)

2 x 400g tins cannellini beans – drained

1 cup (250ml) homemade chicken stock (page 134) or 1 cup hot water

sea salt and pepper

Method

Place the olive oil in a heavy based large saucepan.

Add shallots and gently sauté until translucent.

Add garlic, stir through shallots for 2 minutes.

Add carrot, celery and zucchini, turn up the heat and cook for a few minutes.

Add leek, bacon/pancetta and chilli and all of the herbs.

Stir continuously over a high heat for a few minutes.

Add tomatoes, cannellini beans and tomato paste.

Add the chicken stock or water.

Turn the heat down to a gentle simmer and leave for 40 minutes.

INSPIRATION

This can be eaten anytime, not just for breakfast. Sauté chicken thighs and serve with baked beans and a garden salad.

PERSIAN EGGS

serves 4 - 8

Ingredients

810g tin tomatoes

1 onion – finely chopped

2 teaspoons cumin

2 teaspoons turmeric

free range eggs (amount per person)

fresh parsley

1 fresh chilli – finely diced

oregano

sea salt

Method

In a heavy based saucepan sauté onions until translucent.

Add the cumin, turmeric, oregano and sea salt and mix through.

Add the tomatoes and heat until simmering.

Add the chilli and parsley, stir through.

Gently crack eggs into mixture.

Note – The higher you hold the egg, the deeper it drops into the mixture.

Cook eggs to personal taste.

Serve in bowls with chopped fresh parsley on top.

A COOKED BREAKFAST

serves 2

Ingredients

4 rashers gf bacon

2 gf, df free range chicken sausages

2 handfuls spinach – washed

1 clove garlic – finely chopped

1 teaspoon olive oil

6 cherry tomatoes – halved

1 teaspoon fresh thyme – chopped

4 free range eggs – poached, scrambled or fried

gf baked beans recipe on page 30

Method

Cook meat first by grilling or frying.

In a saucepan, heat oil and add the garlic and tomatoes, sauté for 3 minutes.

Add the english spinach to the garlic and tomatoes and stir until cooked, for about 2 minutes.

Cook eggs to your liking.

Gently arrange ingredients on a plate to serve.

INSPIRATION

Make the light Hollandaise Sauce recipe from page 138 and serve over your cooked breakfast.

SAUSAGE ROAST

INSPIRED BY BILL GRANGER ~ *serves 4*

Ingredients

when chopping ingredients, aim for similar size pieces as they need to be roasted as evenly as possible

6 gf sausages – cut into 4-5 cm pieces

4 vine ripened tomatoes – whole

2 onions – quartered

1 whole head garlic – halved

1 chilli – finely chopped

1 bay leaf

4 carrots – cut into pieces

1 beetroot – cut into pieces

1/2 japanese pumpkin – cut into pieces

1 parsnip – cut into pieces

2 zucchini – cut into pieces

thyme – or any fresh herb

olive oil

sea salt and pepper – to taste

Method

Pre-heat oven to 180C.

Place all ingredients onto an oven tray.

Drizzle with olive oil, sea salt and pepper.

Bake for 1 hour.

BREAKFAST SMOOTHIE

serves 2

Ingredients

1 banana (fresh or frozen)

5 strawberries (fresh or frozen)

1 free range egg

3 tablespoons LSA or nuts of your choice

1/2 tablespoon raw unprocessed honey or
1/2 teaspoon pure maple syrup

1 cup (250ml) gf soymilk

Method

Combine all ingredients in a blender and serve.

CHAI TEA

serves 4

Ingredients

2 cups (500ml) water

1 tea bag or 2 teaspoons – dandelion root,
decaffeinated black / green tea, rooibos

1 small (2cm) piece cinnamon quill

1 cardamom pod

5 cardamom seeds

5 coriander seeds

1/2 bay leaf

1 tablespoon raw unprocessed honey

2 cups (500ml) gf soymilk

Method

*Add water, dandelion root or other tea of
your choice and spices to a small saucepan.*

*Once simmering, add honey and stir gently
until dissolved.*

Let brew for 3 minutes.

*Add milk, stir gently until simmering, strain
and serve.*

INSPIRATION

Add star anise for an aniseed licorice flavour.

~ Snacks ~

Sausage Rolls | Tuna Stacks | Open Kofta with Tzatziki | Almond, Coconut & Carob Balls

PUMPKIN & TUNA SUSHI (RICE FREE)

makes 4 nori rolls

Ingredients – Pumpkin Filling

1 kilo butternut pumpkin – peeled and chopped into pieces

1/2 teaspoon cumin

1/8 teaspoon cardamom

1/8 teaspoon chilli

sea salt and pepper to taste

Method

Steam the pumpkin by placing the pieces in a steaming basket which then sits on top of a saucepan with boiling water in it.

Steam until soft, approximately 30 minutes depending on the size of your pumpkin pieces.

Once soft, place the pumpkin in a clean tea towel.

Wrap the pumpkin tightly in the tea towel and ring out all the moisture.

Place the pumpkin in a bowl and add all the remaining ingredients.

Mix through well and then mash the pumpkin.

Set aside ready to use.

CONTINUED ON NEXT PAGE ...

... continued

Ingredients – Tuna Mix

1 large tin tuna – drained

1 medium spring onion – finely chopped

2 1/2 tablespoons df mayonnaise

sea salt and pepper to taste

Method ... continued

Mix tuna, spring onion, mayonnaise, salt and pepper in a bowl.

Spread a thin layer of pumpkin over one piece of seaweed, leaving 2cm at the top to seal the nori.

Divide tuna mix into 4 portions, add a portion on top of the pumpkin along one side of the nori, about 2cm in from the edge.

Using both hands, gently but firmly roll the seaweed to form a long thin cylinder.

Using a sharp knife, cut along the cylinder at regular intervals to form round pieces, approximately 2cm wide.

Arrange on a dish.

INSPIRATION

Serve with gf, df wasabi and wf tamari.

The Tuna and Egg Salad mixture on page 42 (Inspiration) is also a really good filling for this sushi recipe, together with the pumpkin filling.

CRUNCHY SPICED DHAL

Ingredients

200g moong or mung dhal

1 teaspoon chilli powder

1 teaspoon garam masala

1 teaspoon cumin

olive oil for frying

Method

Place dhal in a bowl and cover with water, soak overnight.

Drain dhal and wrap in muslin cloth or tea towel, leave for 24 hours and it will start to sprout.

Add olive oil to a saucepan, when hot add dhal and fry for approximately 5 minutes until it goes from light yellow to golden and is crunchy.

Drain off oil and place dhal on paper towel.

Season with chilli powder, garam masala and cumin.

INSPIRATION

Buy a plain 200g packet of moong dhal (ready to eat) from asian grocery stores.

Place the moong dhal in a bowl and add 1 teaspoon each of chilli powder, garam masala and cumin.

Mix all the ingredients together and keep in an airtight container ready for snacking.

SPICY LIME NUTS

Ingredients

2 cups mixed nuts and seeds (cashews, almonds, pine nuts, pumpkin seeds)

3 teaspoons allspice

3 teaspoons coriander seeds

1 teaspoon garam masala

1 teaspoon chilli powder

1 teaspoon cumin

2 small limes – juiced

1 teaspoon raw unprocessed honey

1 tablespoon olive oil

Method

Pre-heat oven to 180C.

Place all spices in a dry hot frying pan and stir until fragrant, approximately 1minute.

Place dry spices in a mortar and pestle and grind into a powder.

Heat olive oil in the frying pan.

Add the ground spices.

Add the nuts and seeds and stir until coated.

Add the lime juice while continuing to stir the nuts and seeds.

Add the honey and keep stirring so that the flavours are evenly distributed through the nuts and seeds.

Fry them for 10 minutes.

Place the frying pan in the oven and leave for 5 minutes or until nuts are golden brown.

Remove from the oven and allow to cool.

INSPIRATION

The flavours of this snack can change every time you create it. Choose nuts, seeds and spices that feel right for you. Vary the amounts used depending on how you like things to taste.

TUNA STACKS

Ingredients

1 cucumber – sliced into circles 1/2 cm thick or lettuce leaves

1/2 red onion – finely chopped

3 free range eggs – boiled and mashed

2 stalks celery – finely diced

1 tablespoon lemon juice

1/3 cup walnuts, pine nuts and almonds – roasted

810g tin tuna – drained

4 tablespoons df egg mayonnaise

1/2 punnet cherry tomatoes – quartered

sea salt

Method

In a large bowl combine mayonnaise, lemon juice and sea salt and mix well.

Add red onion, eggs, celery, nuts and tuna – mix to combine.

Cover the tuna mixture and leave in the fridge overnight for the flavours to infuse.

Serve on cucumber slices topped with a quartered cherry tomato or wrap little heaps of the tuna mixture in individual lettuce leaves.

Tuna mixture can be stored in the fridge for up to 3 days.

INSPIRATION

For an Egg and Tuna Salad, omit the cucumber and follow the method adding in the cherry tomatoes. Serve in a bowl lined with lettuce leaves.

CHICKEN PAKODA

makes 24 pieces

Ingredients

500g boneless and skinless free range chicken
– chopped into small cubes

1 onion – finely diced

3 garlic cloves – crushed

2 teaspoons fresh ginger – grated

handful fresh curry leaves – chopped

handful fresh mint leaves – chopped

handful fresh coriander – chopped

2 teaspoons garam masala

1 teaspoon turmeric

1 teaspoon coriander

1 teaspoon cumin

sea salt to taste

1 cup (140g) chickpea flour (besan)

1 free range egg – lightly beaten

oil for deep-frying

Method

Place chicken pieces in a medium saucepan and cook in boiling salted water.

Drain water from chicken.

Place all herbs, spices, flour and chicken pieces in a large bowl and gently mix by hand until everything has a coating of flour.

Add the egg (and extra water if required) until you have a paste-like batter.

Place ping-pong ball sized clumps of batter into the hot oil and deep-fry until dark golden brown.

Serve within a few hours of cooking.

INSPIRATION

If access to fresh herbs is difficult, they can be omitted for a basic chicken nugget dish.

Vegetarian cauliflower option:

Grate a whole cauliflower, omit fresh herbs and chicken pieces and follow the recipe.

Serve with Sambal (page 69).

CHICKEN MEATBALLS

makes 12

Ingredients

1kg chicken mince

2 carrots – grated

2 shallots – finely chopped

6 garlic cloves – finely chopped

1 zucchini – grated

1/2 red capsicum – grated

2 free range eggs

sea salt and pepper

olive oil

Method

Pre-heat oven to 180C.

Add a generous serve of olive oil to a baking tray (you may need 2 baking trays).

Place the tray into the oven to heat the olive oil.

In a frying pan, sauté the shallots and garlic in olive oil for 5 minutes until translucent.

Finely grate the carrots, zucchini and red capsicum.

Add chicken mince and grated vegetables to a large bowl. Whisk the 2 eggs and then add to the chicken and vegetables. Add the garlic and shallots to the chicken and vegetables and sea salt and pepper to taste.

Stir all ingredients until combined.

Using your fingers, take roughly a tablespoon of chicken mixture into the palm of your hand and roll into balls.

Place rolled chicken balls onto the heated baking tray.

Brush the tops of the chicken balls with olive oil (or try a good chilli oil).

Place in the oven and bake for 20 minutes or until golden brown and cooked through.

INSPIRATION

Try adding finely chopped herbs or chilli to the above recipe.

Can be used as a snack or as a main meal with salad or vegetables.

Replace chicken with lamb mince for an alternative.

OPEN KOFTA WITH TZATZIKI

(gluten and dairy free version inspired from MasterChef Australia)

Ingredients – Kofta

1 tablespoon coriander seeds
1 tablespoon cumin seeds
1 tablespoon olive oil
4 french shallots – thinly sliced
4 cloves garlic – thinly sliced
1 bunch coriander – finely chopped
500g lamb or pork mince
rind of 1 lemon – finely grated
1 free range egg
5 tablespoons chickpea flour
gf white corn tortillas
pinch sea salt

Ingredients – Tzatziki

1 lebanese cucumber – finely grated
2 cloves garlic – minced
1/2 lemon – juiced
1 teaspoon olive oil
pinch sea salt
freshly ground pepper
6 mint leaves – chopped
df soy yogurt

Method – Koftas

Fry coriander and cumin seeds until popping and fragrant and then grind them in a mortar and pestle.

Cook shallots and garlic in a frying pan until shallots are translucent.

Allow to cool.

In a medium size bowl combine mince, chickpea flour, lemon rind, egg, coriander, shallots and garlic.

Mix until well combined.

Press mixture onto a corn tortilla leaving a small border around the outer edge.

Cook for 2 minutes in a lightly oiled frying pan. Transfer corn tortilla onto baking tray and place under the grill for 5-6 minutes until cooked and crispy.

Serve with fresh coriander and tzatziki.

Method – Tzatziki

Gently combine all ingredients in a small bowl and serve.

SALT & PEPPER SQUID

Ingredients

1 squid tube per person

gf corn flour or chickpea flour (1 tablespoon for each squid tube used)

good quality sea salt

pepper

oil for frying

lemon wedges

Method

Slice squid tubes into bite size pieces.

Place on paper towels to absorb all the moisture from the squid tubes.

Place squid pieces in a plastic bag.

Add the corn flour, sea salt and pepper to the plastic bag.

Shake the bag until all ingredients are mixed and the squid pieces are coated.

Deep-fry in batches until golden, for about 1 to 2 minutes.

Drain on absorbent paper and serve with lemon wedges.

INSPIRATION

Use salt and chilli instead of salt and pepper.

Try dipping squid into the Aioli Wasabi, see page 140.

CHICKPEA WRAP WITH AVOCADO & BACON

serves 4

Ingredients – Wrap

1 cup (140g) chickpea flour

1 1/4 cups (300ml) water

1 free range egg

1 teaspoon olive oil

Ingredients – Filling

4 tablespoons hummus,
see recipe on page 62

1 avocado – thinly sliced

8 rashers gf bacon – cooked

1 cup (30g) english spinach leaves – chopped

sea salt and pepper

Method

In a medium size mixing bowl, combine all your ingredients and whisk until smooth.

Pre-heat 18cm frying pan on high heat.

Add a drizzle of oil.

Pour a ladle of the mixture so the base is covered.

Wrap is ready to turn when bubbles have appeared and the base comes away easily.

Flip and cook the other side.

Repeat until you have the required amount of wraps.

Fill your wrap by covering one half only with hummus, thinly sliced avocado, one rasher of bacon and english spinach leaves.

Season with sea salt and pepper.

Fold the wraps in half to serve.

INSPIRATION

Use seaweed nori sheets as a wrap instead of the chickpea pancake.

SAUSAGE ROLLS

makes 30 x 6cm rolls

Ingredients – Pastry

180g df margarine

2 cups (250ml) water

2 teaspoons salt

2 1/2 cups (175g) gf flour

1/4 teaspoon (2g) xanthan gum

4 medium free range eggs

1 egg yolk

Method – Pastry

Pre-heat oven to 210C.

In a heavy based saucepan, combine the water, salt and margarine.

Bring to a simmer and add the flour and xanthan gum.

Lower temperature and continue cooking until pastry comes away from the sides and is well combined.

Remove from heat and cool to room temperature.

Whisk eggs and add slowly to flour mix, combine thoroughly.

Knead pastry on a floured surface until smooth and shiny.

Wrap pastry in glad wrap and chill.

Using a rolling pin, roll the pastry between two pieces of baking paper.

Roll to 1/2 cm thickness and 30 cm square if making sausage rolls.

Pastry will keep in the fridge for up to 5 days.

CONTINUED ON NEXT PAGE ...

... continued

Ingredients – Filling

400g gf sausages or free range chicken mince
– you can buy gf sausages and remove the skin

1 large onion – grated

1 carrot – grated

2 tablespoons fresh parsley and chives

sea salt and pepper

2 dessertspoons gf breadcrumbs

Method

Pre-heat oven to 220C.

In a food processor, grate onion, carrot, parsley and chives.

Mix mince, salt and pepper and grated vegetables in a bowl. Add breadcrumbs to mince mixture and combine well.

Place several 30cm pastry squares, 1/2 cm thick on top of the baking paper on your workbench.

Spoon sausage mixture into a piping bag, pipe along one side of the pastry, 2cm in from the edge.

Roll the pastry over the filling until the filling is completely enclosed in pastry.

Cut along the edge of the pastry with a sharp knife.

Repeat the process until you run out of pastry.

Brush rolls with combined cold water and egg yolk.

Cut into desired length, approximately 5 pieces per roll.

Place on baking paper on oven tray and bake in a 220C oven for 20 minutes, reduce heat to 180C and cook for a further 15 minutes (or until sausage rolls are golden brown).

INSPIRATION

Uncooked sausage rolls can be kept in the freezer; simply pull them out and cook when needed.

VIETNAMESE SPRING ROLLS

serves 6

Ingredients

1 packet rice paper, check that they are gf

1 packet gf vermicelli noodles

500g minced free range chicken, pork or turkey or a combination of these

1 tin sliced water chestnuts or chopped peanuts

fresh coriander and vietnamese mint

thinly sliced vegetables of your choice: carrots, green/red capsicums, zucchini, rocket etc

Method – Vietnamese Spring Rolls

Cook vermicelli as per packet instructions.

Fry the mince of your choice and the water chestnuts or peanuts in sesame oil and place in a serving bowl.

On a large serving plate, arrange your selection of thinly sliced vegetables including the mint and coriander.

Place a large bowl with warm water on the table.

Place the noodles and meat on the table for people to help themselves.

To make your vietnamese spring roll, do the following:

Put a rice paper in the bowl of warm water for 30 seconds, remove and place on your plate.

Add your ingredients across the middle of the rice paper.

Gently fold the rice paper over your ingredients, tucking in the sides as you roll it up.

CONTINUED ON NEXT PAGE ...

VIETNAMESE SPRING ROLLS
... continued

Ingredients – Dipping Sauce

1/4 cup (75ml) sesame oil

1/4 cup (75ml) gf fish sauce

1/4 cup (75ml) lime juice

1/4 cup (75ml) gf sweet chilli sauce

1/4 cup mint – chopped

1/4 cup coriander – chopped

1/4 cup fresh chillies – chopped

Method – Dipping Sauce

Mix together sesame oil, fish sauce, mint and coriander, lime juice and sweet chilli sauce (or fresh chillies).

Place in 1 or 2 small bowls on the table for people to dip their rolls into.

INSPIRATION

Use any variation of free range chicken breasts, lamb strips, prawns or tofu in your vietnamese spring rolls.

FRIED SAIGON SPRING ROLLS

Ingredients

500g free range chicken mince

500g prawn meat – minced

1 carrot – grated

1/2 large brown onion – finely diced

1 bunch fresh coriander – chopped

1 free range egg

1 teaspoon sea salt

1 teaspoon ground pepper

vegetable oil – for deep-frying

small size rice paper sheets

INSPIRATION

Serve hot with Dipping Sauce (see page 51), lettuce leaves and fresh herbs.

Freeze any uncooked spring rolls for use later on.

Method

Separate egg yolk and keep the egg white for later.

Take chicken mince, prawn meat, carrot, onion, egg yolk, salt and pepper and mix well in a large bowl.

To assemble the rolls, fill a large bowl with warm water and briefly dip 1 sheet of rice paper at a time in the water. Lay it flat down until the water is absorbed and the rice paper sheet is softened.

Place 1 tablespoon of the filling on the rice paper 3cm from the edge closest to you. Gently fold this edge towards the far end to just cover the filling. Fold the sides into the centre accross the filling and roll from bottom to top to form a tight roll. Use egg white to form a glue to stick the end down.

Pour vegetable oil into a deep frying pan and heat until hot. Cook spring rolls in batches, for 3 to 4 minutes or until golden. Make sure the oil is just covering the spring rolls so they are crispy.

Remove the spring rolls from the pan and place on a plate that is covered with paper towels to absorb the excess oil.

THAI FISH CAKES

makes 12

Ingredients

450g white fish – uncooked

2 tablespoons peanut oil

2 spring onions

2 tablespoons fresh coriander

1 chilli – deseeded

1 tablespoon lime juice

sea salt

2 tablespoons red curry paste

2 cloves garlic

Method

For the fish cakes, whiz together all the ingredients in a food processor. Make sure the mixture remains quite coarse.

Squeeze one dessertspoon of mixture at a time in your hand and shape.

Fry in hot peanut oil, 1 minute each side.

Ingredients – Dipping Sauce

1 small carrot

1 chilli – deseeded

2 lebanese cucumbers – finely chopped

1 tablespoon peanuts – roasted

1 tablespoon wf tamari sauce

1 teaspoon raw unprocessed honey

ginger – 1cm piece

1/2 lemon – juiced

Method – For the sauce

Process the ingredients in a food processor until quite fine.

Place in a small bowl ready to serve with the fish cakes.

APPLE DATE SLICE

serves 8

Ingredients

1 cup (150g) fresh dates –
pitted and chopped

1 cup (250ml) water

1 free range egg – beaten

1 1/2 (165g) cups almond meal

1 cup (65g) shredded coconut

1 cup (125g) pecan halves – chopped (you
can use any nuts of your choice)

1 cup (250ml) gf soymilk

1 free range egg

2 apples – peeled, cored and sliced

Method

Pre-heat oven to 180C.

*Put the dates and water into a pan and bring
to the boil.*

*Cook over medium heat for 5 minutes or until
most of the liquid has been absorbed.*

Transfer the date mixture to a bowl.

*Add the almond meal, coconut (or cooked
quinoa), pecans, soymilk and the egg and mix
to combine.*

*Line a rectangular cake tin (30cm x 20cm)
with baking paper.*

Spoon the mixture into the tin.

*Arrange the sliced apple on top of
the mixture.*

*Bake for 40 minutes or until a skewer comes
out clean.*

INSPIRATION

Replace the dates with semi-dried craisins and blueberries.

Replace coconut with 1 cup (165g) cooked red quinoa.

FRUIT & NUT BALLS

makes 14

Ingredients

8 apricots – chopped

1/2 cup (75g) cashews – pulsed or crushed finely

1/2 cup (55g) almonds – pulsed or crushed finely

3 dessertspoons linseeds – pulsed or crushed finely

3/4 cup (50g) shredded coconut

4 tablespoons raw unprocessed honey

4 tablespoons tahini

desiccated coconut – for coating

Method

Mix all ingredients except the coconut together in a bowl.

Take a spoonful of the mixture at a time and roll into balls.

Roll each ball in desiccated coconut.

INSPIRATION

Remove all dried fruit. Wrap either 1 pear or 1 apple in foil and roast for 40 minutes. Chop into bite sized pieces and add to the finely crushed nuts and continue with the recipe above. Using fresh fruit reduces their shelf life.

ALMOND, COCONUT & CAROB BALLS

makes 12

Ingredients

1 ripe large banana – mashed

4 teaspoons carob powder (use to taste)

1 teaspoon cinnamon

1 1/2 cups (150g) almond or hazelnut meal

1/4 - 1/3 cup (60-80ml) coconut milk

1/3 cup (30g) desiccated coconut

shredded coconut (for coating)

Method

Mix all ingredients together in a large bowl.

Roll into balls and cover with shredded coconut.

Refrigerate for 1/2 hour before serving.

INSPIRATION

Try 100% pure and fresh coconut instead of the desiccated coconut.
You can buy it in asian/indian grocery stores out of the deep freezer.

CHILLED CAROB & NUT SLICE

Ingredients

1/4 cup coconut oil

2 tablespoons carob powder

1/4 cup coconut cream concentrate* or
gf soymilk powder

1/4 cup tahini or nut butter

2 tablespoons raw unprocessed honey

1/4 cup coconut flour

1 cup seeds, nuts or dried fruit

*available from asian grocery stores

Method

In a medium size bowl add coconut oil, carob, coconut cream concentrate, tahini and honey and mix gently with a processor until completely combined.

Gently mix in coconut flour, nuts and seeds.

Line a 20cm x 20cm tin with baking paper, spoon in mixture and chill in fridge until set.

~ Dips ~

Dukkah | Pesto, Beetroot and Hummus Dips

CARROT DIP

Ingredients

4 carrots – cut into chunks

1/2 cup (125ml) water

1/4 cup (63ml) olive oil

1 clove garlic – crushed

1/4 teaspoon oregano

1/4 teaspoon paprika

1/4 teaspoon ground cumin

Method

Place the carrots in a saucepan, cover with water and bring to the boil.

Simmer covered for about 15 minutes or until carrots are tender.

Drain the carrots.

Mix carrots in a bowl with the other ingredients.

Cover and cool.

Blend or process carrot mixture until smooth.

CLASSIC EGGPLANT DIP

Ingredients

1 large eggplant

1/4 cup (63ml) lemon juice

4-5 tablespoons tahini

2 cloves garlic

1 1/2 teaspoons sea salt

fresh parsley – chopped (optional)

Method

Remove the green from around the neck of the eggplant, but leave the stem.

Place in a 180C hot oven until soft (approximately 15-20 minutes).

For a more smoky flavour, wrap in aluminium foil, hold on to stem and place over an open grill or hotplate for about 10 minutes, turning from time to time until the eggplant has softened.

Allow to cool.

Blend thoroughly in a blender while slowly adding lemon juice and tahini.

Crush garlic with salt and mix to a paste and stir into eggplant mixture.

Adjust salt, lemon and tahini to taste.

Garnish with parsley.

HUMMUS

Ingredients

425g chickpeas – canned or freshly soaked
and cooked (see page 128)

1 teaspoon sea salt

2 cloves garlic

1/3 cup (75ml) tahini

juice from 1/3 lemon

paprika to garnish

1/4 cup (63ml) olive oil

Method

Strain chickpeas, keep the juice.

Purée all ingredients in a blender.

Add the juice of the chickpeas until desired consistency is reached.

Serve in a bowl garnished with a pinch of paprika.

INSPIRATION

Add fresh coriander and chilli, and use lime instead of lemon juice.

Add 200g roasted pumpkin.

Prepare a packet of df, gf felafel mix and serve with hummus and salad.

AVOCADO SALSA

Ingredients

1 large avocado – mashed

1 tomato – finely diced

1-2 cloves garlic – crushed

1/2 lemon or lime – juiced

3 tablespoons coriander – chopped

1 red onion – finely diced (optional)

sea salt

Method

Peel and mash the avocado.

Add all other ingredients and gently mix together.

BEETROOT DIP

Ingredients

1 3/4 cup (200g) cashews

1 large beetroot

1 handful basil

1 teaspoon oregano

sea salt

1/2 cup olive oil

Method

Wash the beetroot.

Sit beetroot on a large piece of foil, drizzle with olive oil and sprinkle with sea salt.

Wrap the beetroot in the foil and bake at 180C for 1 hour.

After the beetroot is cooked, place it in a blender.

Add all other ingredients and blend.

TUNA & CANNELLINI DIP

Ingredients

425g canned tuna

425g canned cannellini beans

1/2 lemon – juiced

1/4 cup fresh basil and parsley – chopped

sea salt and pepper

Method

Place all ingredients in a blender and process until smooth.

DUKKAH

Ingredients

1 tablespoon cumin seeds

1 tablespoon fenugreek seeds

2 star anise (optional)

1 tablespoon sesame seeds

1 tablespoon caraway seeds

1 tablespoon mustard seeds

1-3 cardamom pods (not too much)

1 tablespoon dried chillies (optional)

1 tablespoon turmeric (optional)

lots of freshly ground sea salt to taste

Method

Place all ingredients except turmeric in a frypan. Cover and toast until they start to pop and smoke.

Remove from heat and stir well.

Place contents of the saucepan in a mortar.

Add the turmeric and grind to a coarse powder.

INSPIRATION

Dip bread in good olive oil and roll in dukkah. Bread for dunking – use the Almond & Chickpea Pancake (see page 24) or try some of the gf, df and yeast free bread mixes on the market.

Follow the instructions on the packet, let the bread mix rise and then fry in batches in a frying pan. This will produce a naan or foccacia type of gf bread ideal for dipping in oil and dukkah.

PESTO

Ingredients

2 cups (100g) tightly packed basil leaves

2 cloves garlic

1/2 cup (75) pine nuts – toasted

1/2 cup (75g) cashews

1/2 lemon – juiced

sea salt and pepper

olive oil

Method

Place all ingredients in a food processor and blend together.

Add enough olive oil (usually half a cup for a firm pesto) to reach the consistency you desire.

INSPIRATION

You can add different herbs and spices; try coriander, chilli or parsley.

Cashews give the pesto a creamy consistency, as do pine nuts; macademia nuts work very well also.

TOFU, SPINACH & GARLIC DIP

Ingredients

3 cloves garlic

1 chilli

1/4 bunch spinach

1pkt firm silken tofu

2 tablespoons olive oil

Method

Place all ingredients in a blender.

Blend until smooth.

INSPIRATION

Add a handful of rocket to the above recipe.

SAMBAL

Ingredients

1 tablespoon olive oil

1 spanish onion – finely diced

3 cloves garlic – minced

1 shallot – finely sliced

3 chillies – finely diced

¼ teaspoon wf tamari

1 tomato – diced

sea salt and pepper

¼ teaspoon gf fish sauce

1 handful flat leaf parsley – finely chopped

Method

Sauté olive oil, onion, garlic and shallot in a frypan.

Add chillies, tamari and tomato and cook until tomato is softened.

Add salt, pepper and the fish sauce.

Take off the heat and stir through the parsley.

INSPIRATION

Try the Sambal as an accompaniment to Chicken Pakoda (page 43).

~ Salads ~

OBSERVATIONS

When using dressings, make sure they do not contain malt.

Verjuice is a vinegar alternative in dressings. It is made from the unfermented juice of fruit, usually young grapes. Its acid content is around half the concentration of vinegar. Because it is not fermented, there is no yeast content.

Zeleta (Middle Eastern Salad) | Cauliflower Salad | Mango & Cabbage Salad

BROCCOLI & CASHEW SALAD

Ingredients

1 medium broccoli – cut into bite size florets

1/2 cup (60g) cashews

1/2 bunch english spinach – washed

1 red capsicum – diced

Dressing

pinch sea salt

1 teaspoon lemon juice

4 tablespoons df mayonnaise

2 tablespoons mild curry powder

1 teaspoon paprika

Method

Place the cashews on a baking tray and roast in the oven at 150C until golden.

Lightly blanch broccoli in boiling water for two minutes. Remove the broccoli from the pot and place in ice-cold water to stop the cooking process.

Drain the broccoli.

Combine all salad ingredients in a salad bowl.

Mix dressing ingredients together in a small jug.

Dress salad just before serving.

QUINOA TABBOULEH

Ingredients

3/4 cup (150g) red quinoa

1 cup (250ml) water

4 tomatoes – diced

2 sticks celery – diced

2 cucumbers – peeled and diced

2 bunches flat leaf parsley – coarsely chopped

2 spring onions – finely sliced

Dressing

6 tablespoons olive oil

juice of 2 lemons

6 tablespoons wf tamari

Method

Place water and red quinoa in a saucepan.

Cover with a lid and bring to the boil.
Turn the heat down to low and cook for another 15-20 minutes.

Check if there is any water left in the saucepan by tipping the pot on an angle, five minutes before the end of cooking time. If there is, continue to cook until no liquid remains. When it is ready, small steam holes should appear on the surface.

Transfer into serving bowl and leave to cool.

Prepare your vegetables and the parsley.

Whisk together the dressing ingredients.

Add vegetables to cooled red quinoa, add dressing and serve.

SIMPLE GREEN SALAD

Ingredients

1 cup (43g) baby spinach leaves

1 cup (43g) rocket

1 cup (43g) cos lettuce

1/2 cup (85g) sesame seeds, slivered almonds or pine nuts

2 tablespoons wf tamari

Method

Lightly roast your choice of nuts in tamari in a frying pan.

Combine all the salad ingredients in a separate bowl.

Toss the roasted nuts or seeds gently over your bowl of salad greens and serve.

INSPIRATION

You can use the Citrus Salad Dressing (page 141) instead of the tamari dressing.

MANGO & CABBAGE SALAD

Ingredients

1/4 white cabbage – diced

2 small or 1 large mango – sliced

1 bunch coriander – chopped

1 bunch vietnamese mint – finely chopped

3 spring onions – finely sliced

carrots – julienned (cut into long thin strips)

Dressing

50ml seasame oil

50ml gf fish sauce

50ml gf sweet chilli sauce

Method

Prepare vegetables and place in a salad bowl.

Prepare the salad dressing.

Dress the vegetables gently and serve immediately.

ASIAN SLAW

Ingredients

2 tablespoons black or white sesame seeds – toasted

1/2 medium (500-750g) head napa cabbage (chinese cabbage)

1 medium carrot

4 spring onions

Dressing

2 tablespoons wf tamari

2 tablespoons verjuice

1 teaspoon sesame oil

1 tablespoon lime juice (half a lime)

1 teaspoon fresh ginger – grated

1 pinch cayenne

sea salt and pepper to taste

Method

Toast sesame seeds in a dry frying pan over low heat until fragrant. Set aside to cool.

Cut the cabbage head into quarters lengthwise and remove the core.

Slice each quarter into very fine strips.

Peel and julienne the carrot.

Remove root ends of spring onions and slice white and green parts thinly.

Toss the cabbage, carrot and spring onion together.

In a small bowl, whisk together tamari, verjuice, sesame oil, lime juice, ginger and cayenne.

Pour the dressing over the vegetables ten minutes before serving. Add the toasted sesame seeds and gently mix through.

Serve immediately or store in the refrigerator until ready to serve.

INSPIRATION

For an alternative, try the Sweet Asian Dressing (page 142).

ZELETA (MIDDLE EASTERN SALAD)

Ingredients

4 large firm tomatoes – diced

1 large cucumber – diced

1 green capsicum – diced

1 red capsicum – diced

1 bunch coriander or parsley – chopped

1 small spanish onion – diced

400g chickpeas – drained
(freshly cooked or canned)

1 lemon – juiced

sea salt and pepper to taste

Method

Place all diced and chopped salad ingredients in a bowl together with the drained chickpeas.

Add sea salt and pepper to taste.

Add the lemon juice.

Gently mix all ingredients together and serve.

ROASTED CORN SALAD

Ingredients

3 corn cobs

1 avocado – chopped

350g cherry tomatoes – halved

2 tablespoons lime or lemon juice

1/4 cup (20g) coriander – chopped

1/2 teaspoon sesame oil

Method

Roast corn under the grill.

Trim corn kernels off the cob.

Add all ingredients to a salad bowl.

Mix together gently and serve.

CAULIFLOWER SALAD

Ingredients

1 medium cauliflower – cut into pieces

3 cloves garlic – finely chopped

1/2 - 1 bunch parsley – finely chopped

2 tablespoons white sesame seeds

2 tablespoons black sesame seeds

black pepper and sea salt

4 tablespoons olive oil

Method

Steam cauliflower until a knife slides through the pieces easily.

Place the cooked cauliflower into a dish.

Fry the garlic, black pepper and parsley in olive oil for two minutes.

Add the sesame seeds and fry for another minute.

Pour the garlic, parsley and sesame seeds over the cauliflower.

Sprinkle with sea salt.

Serve hot or cold.

~ Soups ~

OBSERVATIONS

It is worth getting a good quality sea salt to use instead of pre-made stocks.

Use sea vegetables such as kombu, arame and wakame as a base to flavour soups, stocks and stews. They are nutrient rich and bring out the flavours of the food.

If you do not have a gf, wf and df stock available, then sauté a leek and some celery in oil and use this before starting any soup.

Most pre-made stocks contain gluten or wheat or lactose and yeast. So remember to read your labels carefully.

Vietnamese Pho Ga | Pumpkin Soup | Gazpacho | Green Curry Chicken Chowder

VIETNAMESE PHO GA

serves 10

Ingredients – Broth

2 free range chickens

5 litres water

5 french shallots – peeled and left whole

2 x 8 cm pieces fresh ginger – unpeeled

1 1/2 tablespoons salt

3 tablespoons gf fish sauce

1 tablespoon raw unprocessed honey

2 tablespoons coriander seeds

4 whole cloves

2 tablespoons fennel seeds

5 star anise

1 cinnamon stick

700g small flat rice stick noodles

Ingredients – Garnishes

3 cups bean sprouts

10 to 12 sprigs fresh mint

10 to 12 sprigs fresh thai basil

12 to 15 fresh coriander leaves

2 or 3 thai red chillies – thinly sliced

2 or 3 limes or lemons - cut into wedges

CONTINUED ON NEXT PAGE ...

... continued

Method

Fry all spices in a pan until aroma is released – avoid burning.

Wrap spices in a piece of cheese cloth and tie off into a spice bag.

Place the shallots and ginger on a baking tray and grill on high heat for 15 minutes until charred, softened and sweet. Let cool.

Gently rub off any blackened bits and halve ginger lengthwise.

Rinse the chicken under cool water and remove the wings.

Parboil all the chicken by placing them in a 12 litre pot with cold water until just covered.

Bring to a boil over high heat and boil vigorously for 2 to 3 minutes.

Discard the water and rinse the chickens to get rid of any residue; put them back into a clean stock pot.

Add 5 litres of water and bring to the boil, then reduce heat to a gentle simmer.

Add the shallots, ginger, salt, fish sauce, raw unprocessed honey and spice bag and simmer uncovered for 40 minutes.

Remove chickens and run under cold water, let them cool down enough to handle – keep the broth at a gentle simmer and top up with boiling water if necessary.

Use a knife to remove each chicken breast and the whole legs (thigh and drumstick) and any other meat you wish. Set aside to completely cool for shredding.

Return the leftover carcasses to the stock pot and adjust the heat to simmer the broth gently for another 1 1/2 hours.

Once the meat is cool, shred or cut it into the size you want for your soup. Keep your eyes on the broth and remove any scum that appears on the top.

Strain the broth into a saucepan, discarding the carcasses.

Assemble the Pho bowls. If using noodles, cook them in a separate saucepan with water, oil and salt until just tender.

Prepare all the garnishes and place them on a plate for the table.

Ladle broth, noodles and chicken into bowls.

Let each person garnish their own bowl as they feel to.

PUMPKIN SOUP

serves 6 - 8

Ingredients

5.5 cups (1kg) pumpkin – peeled and chopped

2 tablespoons oil

1 spanish red onion – chopped

4 cups (1l) water

salt and pepper

3/4 cup (190ml) df, gf milk (optional)

handful fresh basil – finely chopped

Method

Pre-heat oven to 180C.

Peel and chop pumpkin.

Place pumpkin on a lightly oiled baking tray and bake until soft.

In a large saucepan, sauté onion until translucent.

Add sea salt, pumpkin and water and cook for 20 minutes.

Process in a blender until smooth.

Stir in milk if you are using it.

Serve topped with fresh basil.

INSPIRATION

After blending the soup, add some crushed macadamias and fresh corn kernels.

FRESH TOMATO SOUP

serves 6

Ingredients

8 roma tomatoes – diced

2 whole heads of garlic

1 onion – diced

425g can crushed tomatoes

1 tablespoon oil

4 cups (1l) water

sea salt to taste

handful fresh parsley – chopped

Method

Heat oven to 180C.

Place whole garlic on a baking tray and roast for 20 minutes until the flesh is soft.

In a large saucepan, add oil and sauté onion gently until translucent.

Add roma tomatoes and cook for 20 minutes.

Add the roasted garlic flesh to the saucepan by squeezing the cloves of garlic gently out of their skins.

Add water, tinned tomatoes and roasted garlic flesh and let simmer for 20 minutes.

Serve with fresh parsley.

VEGETABLE SOUP

serves 6 - 8

Ingredients

1 whole garlic – roasted
1 onion – peeled and diced
200g pumpkin – peeled and diced
1 carrot – peeled and diced
200g sweet potato – peeled and diced
1 leek – sliced
2 celery sticks – diced
1 zucchini – diced
1 tablespoon oil
2 litres water
450g of your favourite beans or legumes
1 teaspoon mild curry powder
1 teaspoon turmeric
810g can crushed tomatoes
410g can creamed corn
handful fresh herbs
salt and pepper

Method

Pre-heat oven to 180C.

Bake whole garlic in its skin in the oven for 15 minutes or until squishy, set aside to cool.

In a large saucepan, add the oil and sauté the leek and celery until leek is translucent.

Add all other vegetables, sauté for 10 minutes.

Remove garlic from the skin by squeezing it, add to the saucepan.

Add curry powder, turmeric and fresh herbs to sautéed vegetables and cook for 3 minutes.

Add the legumes, crushed tomatoes and creamed corn.

Add water to just cover the vegetables.

Bring to the boil, reduce the heat, cover and simmer for 20 minutes.

Add sea salt and pepper to taste.

For a smoother soup, process in a blender.

INSPIRATION

Roast all vegetables and follow the recipe.

You can also add left-over roasted meats to this soup.

GREEN CURRY CHICKEN CHOWDER

serves 4

Ingredients

1 sweet potato – peeled and diced

2 fresh corn cobs – kernels removed

1 tablespoon sunflower oil

2 tablespoons gf green curry paste

2 free range chicken breasts – thinly sliced

400ml can coconut milk

1/2 cup (125ml) water

2 limes – zest and juice

3 kaffir lime leaves

2 teaspoons gf fish sauce

1 chilli – finely sliced

1 cup thai basil – finely chopped

1 cup coriander – finely chopped

Method

For a crunchy texture, steam the sweet potato until tender. Add corn kernels when you add the chicken.

Heat the oil in a large saucepan over medium heat.

Add the curry paste, stirring and cooking for 30 seconds.

Stir in chicken, coconut milk, stock, lime zest and juice, kaffir lime leaves and simmer for 10-15 minutes.

Add the sweet potato and corn kernels and cook 1-2 minutes.

Add fish sauce.

Ladle chowder into bowls.

Place sliced and chopped chilli, thai basil and coriander in small serving bowls for everyone to add to their chowder as they feel to.

GAZPACHO (SPANISH COLD SOUP)

serves 8

Ingredients

1 spanish red onion

3 tomatoes

1/2 medium cucumber

1/2 green capsicum

1/2 red capsicum

3 cloves garlic – crushed

3 1/2 cups (875ml) tomato juice

sea salt and pepper to taste

1/4 cup (63ml) olive oil

1/4 cup (63ml) verjuice

Method

Finely chop onion, tomatoes, cucumber, capsicum and place in a large bowl with the garlic.

Stir in tomato juice and verjuice.

Add oil and sea salt, pepper to taste.

Refrigerate and serve cold.

INSPIRATION

Grill two corn cobs for 20 minutes turning them regularly. Remove kernels and add to the soup or gently roast frozen or tinned corn in a frying pan with a little oil until golden.

CELERIAC & SPINACH SOUP

serves 6

Ingredients

2 tablespoons extra virgin olive oil

1 leek – thinly sliced

2 french shallots – thinly sliced

3 garlic cloves – crushed

1 celeriac (700g) – peeled and grated

1 litre boiling water

1 bay leaf

500g english spinach leaves –
washed and stems removed

1 teaspoon nutmeg – grated

sea salt

pepper

parsley or chives to garnish – finely chopped

Method

*Heat the oil in a large saucepan
on gentle heat.*

*Add the leek, shallots and garlic,
cook for 5 minutes or until the leek and
shallots are translucent.*

*Add the celeriac and bay leaf and cook for
a further 5 minutes.*

*Pour in the boiling water and bring to the
boil over a high heat, reduce the heat and
cover the saucepan.*

*Cook the soup gently for 15 minutes or
until the celeriac is tender.*

Add the spinach to the soup and stir well.

*Increase the heat and bring the soup to the
boil until spinach has softened, add nutmeg,
remove from heat.*

*Purée soup in batches, with a blender or
food processor until smooth.*

Reheat adding salt and pepper.

Garnish with fresh parsley or chives.

CHICKEN & CORN SOUP

serves 6

Ingredients

6 cups (1.5l) water

440g can creamed corn

500g free range chicken mince

2 free range egg whites

3 tablespoons gf corn flour

1 handful mung bean sprouts

2 teaspoons sesame oil

2 tablespoons wf tamari

sea salt to taste

Method

Place chicken mince in a small bowl, add egg whites and let sit for 10 minutes.

In a medium saucepan, add water, creamed corn, sesame oil, tamari and sea salt, bring to the boil.

Add chicken mince, bring back to the boil and simmer for 5 minutes.

Add corn flour to 1/4 cup of water and blend to a paste.

Add corn flour mixture to soup when simmering.

Cook and keep stirring until soup thickens.

Top with bean sprouts.

~ Mains ~

Crumbed Fish | Simple Mediterranean Chicken | Pork Stir Fry with Noodles | Roast Chicken

GADO GADO

serves 4

Ingredients – Peanut Sauce

1/2 cup (80g) onions – diced

2 cloves garlic – minced

1 bay leaf

1 teaspoon oil

1/2 teaspoon turmeric

1 cup (250ml) crunchy peanut butter or any nut paste

1 tablespoon raw unprocessed honey

1/2 teaspoon cayenne pepper

1 lemon – juiced

1 teaspoon fresh ginger – grated

1 tablespoon lemon juice or verjuice

2 cups (500ml) water

1 tablespoon wf tamari

1 tablespoon gf fish sauce

Method

see page over ...

CONTINUED ON NEXT PAGE ...

... continued

Ingredients – Salad Base

800g sweet potato – peeled and cut
into 4cm cubes

4 free range eggs – boiled and halved

1/2 savoy cabbage – finely shredded

1 carrot – sliced lengthways

1 cup baby beans – chopped in half

1 lebanese cucumber – sliced lengthways

1 cup (130g) mung bean sprouts

1 fresh chilli – diced

Method

Prepare all of the salad base ingredients.

Steam sweet potatoes until tender.

To prepare the peanut sauce:

Add one teaspoon of oil, diced onion, minced garlic and bay leaf to a small saucepan, cook until onions are soft and remove from heat.

Add peanut butter or other nut paste, honey, cayenne pepper, lemon juice, ginger, water, tamari and fish sauce, and gently whisk together.

Return saucepan to heat and simmer for 15-20 minutes.

Arrange salad on a platter in the order of the ingredients list.

When ready to serve, pour the warm sauce over the top.

Sprinkle with chilli.

COCONUT CHICKEN & ASIAN SALAD

serves 4

Ingredients

4 free range chicken breasts

270ml coconut milk

1/4 chinese cabbage – finely shredded

10 snow peas – finely sliced

75g sprouts (choose from broccoli, mung bean, snow pea)

1/2 cup (25g) coriander – finely chopped

1/2 cup (25g) arame (sea vegetable) – optional

Ingredients – Dressing

1/2 cup (125ml) coconut milk

6 teaspoons lemon juice, lime juice or verjuice

3 teaspoons umeboshi vinegar (plum vinegar)

1 tablespoon apple concentrate or raw unprocessed honey

3 tablespoons sesame oil

1 tablespoon ginger – finely grated

Method

Soak arame in boiling water for 15 minutes.

Place chicken breasts in a saucepan, add coconut milk and water until just covered. Gently simmer for 10 minutes (cooking time will vary depending on the size).

Remove chicken breasts from saucepan.

Immediately shred the meat with a fork.

Place all dressing ingredients in a small bowl and mix well.

Add cabbage, snow peas, sprouts and coriander to a large salad bowl.

Drain arame and add to the salad, mix thoroughly.

Add chicken meat and serve with dressing.

MIXED DHAL

serves 6

Ingredients

1/2 cup (100g) toor dhal – yellow split peas

1/2 cup (100g) masoor dhal – red lentils

1/2 cup (100g) moong dhal –
split moong beans

2 tablespoons oil

3 teaspoons black mustard seeds

1/2 teaspoon black onion seeds (kalonji)

2 medium onions (300g) – chopped

4 cloves garlic – crushed

1 tablespoon fresh ginger – grated

1 tablespoon ground cumin

3 teaspoons ground coriander

1 teaspoon ground turmeric

1 teaspoon chilli powder

800g can crushed tomatoes

2 1/2 cups (625ml) water or vegetable stock
(page 135)

2 tablespoons fresh coriander – chopped

1 sprig curry leaves

Method

Rinse each dhal separately under cold water and then drain.

Put only the toor dhal in a bowl, cover with water and soak for 30 minutes and then drain.

Heat the oil in a pan and cook mustard seeds and black onion seeds until they pop and then add the onions, garlic and ginger.

Add the ground cumin, coriander and turmeric and cook for 1 minute.

Add all the dhal, crushed tomatoes and stock.

Simmer for about 30 minutes or until the red lentils are tender. Add curry leaves.

Just before serving, add chilli, black cracked pepper and fresh coriander. Stir over low heat until just heated through.

INSPIRATION

Cooked fish and chicken can be added to the dhal; stir through just before serving.

PESTO CHICKEN

serves 4

Ingredients

8 free range chicken thighs

1/4 cup olive oil

4 cloves garlic – finely diced

1/2 cup (125ml) pesto (page 67)

Method

Marinate chicken thighs with olive oil and garlic in a bowl for 15 minutes. Make sure you have gently coated all the chicken with the olive oil and garlic.

Add the pesto to the marinade, gently coating all surfaces again.

Place chicken on a baking tray and cook in the oven for 40 minutes or until chicken is tender.

Serve with the simple green salad (page 74) or zeleta (page 77).

CRUMBED FISH

serves 4 - 6

Ingredients

2 free range eggs

1 tablespoon wf tamari

1 cup (130g) gf breadcrumbs

oil for frying

4 large firm fish fillets

1 clove garlic – crushed

1 teaspoon curry powder (optional)

sea salt and pepper

Method

Place the eggs and tamari in a bowl and whisk together.

Put the breadcrumbs, garlic and curry powder in a separate bowl.

Slice fish into even portions and dunk in the egg mixture and then roll in the breadcrumbs.

Heat oil in frying pan, add the fish and cook in batches until done.

Drain on absorbent paper.

INSPIRATION

*You can leave the gf breadcrumbs plain or add a combination of the following:
zest from 1 lemon, pinch of sea salt and pepper to taste,
1/4 cup (10g) finely chopped flat leaf parsley.*

POLENTA COATED PATTIES

makes 20

Ingredients

415g can tuna – drained

415g can red salmon – drained

1 large onion – finely chopped

1 sweet potato – cooked and mashed or finely grated

440g can brown lentils – drained

1 large free range egg or 2 small free range eggs – beaten

1/2 cup (25g) fresh parsley or any fresh herb – finely chopped

2 teaspoons curry powder

dash olive oil

1 cup (225g) polenta

Method

Heat oven to 180C.

Fry onion until translucent.

Mix all ingredients together, except the polenta.

Form mixture into patties and coat with uncooked polenta.

Place patties on a tray brushed with oil.

Brush the tops of the patties with oil.

Bake in the oven for 20-30 minutes.

GARLIC PRAWNS

serves 4

Ingredients

1 kg large prawns – shelled, tails left on
or taken off

1/2 cup olive oil

8 garlic gloves – finely chopped

1/2 lemon – juiced

1 cup flat leaf parsley – finely chopped

Method

2 HOURS BEFORE COOKING, place olive oil, garlic and lemon juice in a small container with a lid. With the lid on, give the container a really good shake.

Place the container in the freezer and allow to almost freeze.

Pre-heat the oven to 180C.

Arrange the prawns in an ovenproof dish.

Remove the container from the freezer and place the mixture on top of the prawns. You can gently break this into pieces and scatter over the prawns or leave as a solid mass.

Place prawns in the oven and bake for 15 minutes.

Serve directly out of the ovenproof dish for people to help themselves.

Serve with a simple green salad and use the run-off garlic sauce as a dressing (if there is any left over from the prawns).

Top with fresh flat leaf parsley.

ROAST CHICKEN

serves 4 - 6

Ingredients

medium sized free range chicken

1 cup mixed fresh herbs – oregano, marjoram, thyme

1 sprig rosemary

1 bay leaf

lemon

head garlic – left whole

3-4 shallots – peeled

extra virgin olive oil

sea salt

pepper

For a quick gravy

Drain all the liquid from the roasting tray and add 100ml chicken stock to a saucepan over a high heat and start to reduce. Add fresh herbs, a touch of salt and pepper and when the consistency feels right, pour into a small jug and serve alongside the roast chicken.

CONTINUED ON NEXT PAGE ...

Method

2 HOURS BEFORE COOKING, pick the oregano, marjoram and thyme leaves until you have approximately 1 cup.

Put half the herbs in a small container and add enough olive oil to cover.

Add a touch of salt and pepper and put in the freezer.

Pre-heat the oven to 200C.

Clean the chicken by running it under cold water, letting the water wash through the cavity and over the skin as well.

Pat the chicken dry inside and out with kitchen paper.

Sprinkle the inside with sea salt and a grind or three of pepper.

Put the chicken on a baking / roasting tray.

Take the container of herbs and olive oil from the freezer, it should be firm but not frozen.

To get the herbs and oil under the breast skin, gently place your fingers under the skin and push along close to the breast meat to create a pocket over each chicken breast.

... continued

Gently start pushing the herbs and olive oil into the 2 pockets, being careful not to tear the skin.

Roll the lemon back and forth under the palm of your hand until you feel it give to release the juice.

Slice the lemon in half, insert it into the cavity of the chicken with the sliced side facing in, squeeze out all the juice and leave the spent lemon in place at the back of the cavity.

Insert the bay leaf and sprig of rosemary and add the second lemon half, sliced side facing into the cavity, squeezing out all of the juice into the chicken. This lemon half stays in the cavity opening.

Either side of the cavity there should be a flap of skin, take a sharp knife and make a cut, just big enough to push a leg through.

Do not cut too near the edge otherwise it will tear. Now bring the other leg across and push this through the same hole, essentially creating a wrap for both legs to close over the cavity.

Take a very sharp knife and make two diagonal cuts on the meat of each leg so it cooks together with the rest of the chicken.

Rub all of the skin and fill the incisions on the legs with olive oil, sprinkle with sea salt and pepper and the rest of the herbs.

Put the chicken in the oven at 200C for 1/2 hour.

Peel the shallots. After 1/2 hour, take out the tray, add shallots and the head of garlic together with a splash of olive oil, turn down the oven to 180C and cook for approximately one hour.

Keep checking on the shallots and garlic and remove if they look done, leaving the chicken to completely cook.

Remove chicken from the oven, cover with aluminum foil and place in a warm spot, allow to rest for 15 to 20 minutes.

Assemble the other parts of the roast, carve and serve with the roasted head of garlic and the shallots.

CHICKEN SCHNITZEL

serves 4 - 6

Ingredients

1 cup (130g) gf breadcrumbs
(for the best result, use bread rather than
rice crumbs)

rind of 1 lemon – finely grated

good pinch sea salt

pepper to taste

1/4 cup (10g) fresh flat leaf parsley –
chopped finely

2 cloves garlic – finely chopped

olive oil for frying

4 free range chicken breasts –
sliced into portions

Method

Place the breadcrumbs, lemon rind, sea salt, pepper and parsley in a large bowl and combine thoroughly.

Roll chicken portions in the mixture.

Heat olive oil in frying pan, add garlic cloves and cook the chicken breasts in batches until done.

(The garlic cloves add a bit of extra flavour without overpowering the dish.)

INSPIRATION

Replace gf breadcrumbs with crushed macadamia nuts.

CHILLI CON CARNE

serves 6

Ingredients

2 medium onions – chopped

1 clove garlic

olive oil

2 level teaspoons chilli powder

1 heaped teaspoon cumin – ground

sea salt

2 heaped teaspoons coriander – ground

1 heaped teaspoon paprika

500g minced lamb

1 medium green capsicum – finely diced

1 medium red capsicum – finely diced

1 stick cinnamon

160g sun-dried tomatoes in olive oil

1 fresh red chilli – finely chopped

400g canned chopped tomatoes

1/2 cup (125ml) water

200g can red kidney beans – drained

sea salt to taste

Method

Pre-heat oven to 150C degrees.

In a heavy based frying pan that can be used in the oven, place onions and garlic and sauté in olive oil until translucent.

Add the chilli powder and all spices. Add the meat to the pan and cook until slightly browned, add red and green capsicums and cinnamon stick.

Place the sun-dried tomatoes with the oil and chilli in the processor and blend into a paste.

Add the paste to the minced lamb, add the tomatoes and water, drained kidney beans and sea salt to taste.

Bring to the boil on the stovetop, turn the heat down to simmer and cook for 1 hour or transfer the pan to the oven and cook for 1 hour.

SIMPLE MEDITERRANEAN CHICKEN

serves 4

Ingredients

1 tablespoon olive oil

4 free range chicken breasts

3/4 cup (100g) kalamata olives – pitted

2 big handfuls fresh basil – chopped

1 lemon – rind finely grated and juiced

3 cloves garlic – crushed

sea salt

Method

Pre-heat oven to 190C.

Pour olive oil into the base of a medium baking dish.

Gently arrange the chicken breasts on top.

Sprinkle with half the basil leaves and all of the olives, lemon juice, lemon rind and sea salt.

Gently toss ingredients with fingers.

Place in the oven and cook for 20-25 minutes.

Mix through remaining basil and serve.

PORK STIR FRY WITH NOODLES

serves 4

Ingredients

500g minced pork

425g tin asian vegetables – bamboo shoots,
baby corn, bean sprouts

55g fresh broccoli – cut into florets

6 fresh snow peas – julienned

1 chilli – chopped

1 tablespoon garlic – minced

2 tablespoons wf tamari

1 teaspoon agave nectar

1 packet vermicelli glass noodles

1/2 cup fresh coriander – chopped

1 cup fresh bean sprouts

Method

In a wok or large saucepan, add the oil and cook the ginger, garlic and pork mince for 5 minutes or until brown.

Add vegetables, tamari and agave nectar.

When vegetables are cooked to your liking, remove and gently stir through fresh sprouts and coriander.

Cook noodles according to the instructions on the packet.

Place noodles on a long serving plate and top with the pork stir fry.

INSPIRATION

For a noodle free pork stir fry, fry half a finely diced cabbage and 3 finely chopped garlic cloves in olive oil.

Add 1 finely grated carrot and zucchini and cook for 5 minutes.

Add 2 tablespoons gf fish sauce.

Add 500g pork mince and stir fry for 10 minutes or until mince is cooked.

ELEVEN VEG SHEPHERD'S PIE

serves 6

Ingredients – Pie

500g lamb, pork or chicken mince

1 tablespoon olive oil

1 medium onion – finely chopped

1 bay leaf

stringless beans – diced

1 cup (160g) peas and corn
(fresh, frozen or tinned)

1 carrot – diced

1/2 cup (180g) broccoli – in florets

1/2 zucchini – diced

1/2 cup (120g) cauliflower – diced

810g tin chopped tomatoes

1 tablespoon mild curry powder

400g tin lentils – drained

1 teaspoon turmeric

sea salt to taste

Ingredients – Mash Topping

1 sweet potato – peeled and chopped

1 cup (190g) pumpkin –
peeled and chopped

1 tablespoon olive oil

Method

Pre-heat oven to 180C.

Steam sweet potato and pumpkin until soft.

Drain off water and mash, add oil and put aside.

Add a tablespoon of oil to a saucepan or ovenproof dish, add onion, curry powder and turmeric, cook until translucent and soft.

Add bay leaf and mince and cook until just browned.

Add the beans, peas, corn, carrot, broccoli, zucchini and cauliflower. Lightly sauté for 5 minutes.

Add tinned tomatoes and bring back to a simmer.

Add the lentils.

Place mixture in an ovenproof dish and top with sweet potato and pumpkin mash.

Place dish in oven and cook for 45 minutes, finish with 5 minutes under the grill to make the topping crispy.

SEAFOOD STEW

serves 4

Ingredients

1 tablespoon olive oil

4 spring onions – finely chopped

2 cloves garlic – crushed

1 red chilli – finely chopped

10 ripe tomatoes – seeded and chopped finely

1 piece kombu (10cm)

20g arame – soaked in warm water for 15 minutes, drained

20g wakame – soaked in warm water for 15 minutes, drained

1 cup (250ml) verjuice

1 cup (250ml) vegetable stock (page 131)

300g firm fish – cut into chunks

100g clams or scallops

24 mussels – debearded

12 prawns – shelled

100g squid tubes – cut into quarters

handful fresh basil

handful fresh flat leaf parsley

Method

Pre-heat oven to 180C.

Add oil to a large casserole dish with a lid and place in oven to heat for 5 minutes.

Add spring onions and sauté in oven for 5 minutes.

Add garlic and chilli, sauté in oven for 5 minutes.

Add tomatoes and kombu and cook in oven until juice is released, about 25-30 minutes.

Add verjuice and vegetable stock and simmer for 10 minutes.

Add seafood, wakame and arame, stir gently and cook for 10-15 minutes.

Remove kombu if it has not dissolved.

Serve topped with fresh basil and flat leaf parsley.

PASTA FREE CHICKEN LASAGNE

serves 6

Ingredients – Filling

1 onion – diced

2 cloves garlic – chopped

1 red capsicum – diced

500g free range chicken mince

400g tin creamed corn

1 packet frozen english spinach – defrosted

2 free range eggs – hard boiled

150g packet silken tofu – mashed

3 eggplants or 3 large zucchini – sliced and grilled

400g can chopped tomatoes

sea salt and pepper to taste

Method – Filling

Pre-heat oven to 180C

Grill eggplant or zucchini and put aside.

Fry the onions, garlic and capsicum until soft and remove from the pan.

Brown the chicken mince.

Return onions, garlic and capsicum to the pan.

Add the creamed corn, spinach, boiled eggs and tofu.

Mix together until well combined.

Season with sea salt and pepper.

CONTINUED ON NEXT PAGE ...

PASTA FREE CHICKEN LASAGNE

... continued

Ingredients – Sauce

1/3 cup (50g) gf flour

1/3 cup (50g) df margarine

300-350ml gf, df milk – warmed

pepper and salt

pinch of nutmeg

Method – Sauce

In a saucepan, melt the margarine and stir in the flour to form a roux.

Return to heat and gradually add the warmed milk, stirring all the time.

Simmer for approximately 2-3 minutes.

If the sauce is too thick, add a little more milk.

Add nutmeg and pepper and salt.

ASSEMBLE

Place a thin layer of olive oil on the bottom of the lasagna dish.

Spread a layer of eggplant or zucchini slices across.

Add half the chicken filling.

Spread a layer of white sauce over the chicken followed by another layer of eggplant or zucchini slices.

Add the second half of the chicken filling and then more white sauce.

Top with a layer of eggplant or zucchini slices.

Cover with the tomatoes.

Bake in a moderate oven at 180C for 45 minutes.

EGGPLANT STEW

serves 4

Ingredients

2 medium eggplants -- sliced and salted

2 small onions – diced

500g lamb steak – diced

810g tin crushed tomatoes

2 tablespoons turmeric

sea salt and pepper

Preparation

3 HOURS BEFORE COOKING THE EGGPLANT, peel and cut into 2cm wide slices.

Place eggplant slices on paper towel.

Sprinkle generously with salt all over and leave to sweat for at least 2 hours.

After 2 hours, dab eggplant with paper towels to absorb the liquid.

Method

Turn oven to 220C.

Brush eggplant with vegetable oil, place on a baking tray and put in oven.

Allow to cook for 25 minutes or until eggplant is soft.

In a medium saucepan, fry the onion in olive oil until translucent.

Add the meat to brown.

Add turmeric, some sea salt and pepper to taste.

Add crushed tomatoes and cooked eggplant.

Simmer for 30 minutes.

Serve with Crunchy Garlic Brown Rice (page 124).

This dish freezes really well.

PAD THAI

serves 4 - 6

Method

Soak noodles in lukewarm water for 5-10 minutes, until they just soften.

In a small saucepan, combine fish sauce, palm sugar and tamarind pulp and simmer on low heat until sugar is dissolved.

Taste the sauce so you have the right balance of sweet, salty and sour.

Remove from heat and keep aside, ready to use.

Heat a large wok on high until smoky.

Add 4 tablespoons oil.

Add sliced chicken until half cooked.

Add tofu, garlic and spring onion.

Add 2 tablespoons of sauce and stir through.

Drain rice stick noodles and add to wok.

Add 1/4 cup of sauce stirring constantly to stop ingredients from sticking.

Add water if liquid evaporates too quickly.

When the noodles are ready, push to one side and crack the egg in the middle, cook 15 seconds and toss through the noodles.

Taste the noodles to make sure they are cooked.

Add prawns and bean sprouts. Add more sauce if it looks pale.

Serve with lime wedges and peanuts.

Ingredients

1/2 cup (125ml) gf fish sauce

1/4 cup (50g) palm sugar or apple concentrate

1/2 cup (125ml) tamarind pulp

500g thai rice stick noodles (1-2 loosely packed cups per portion)

4 tablespoons oil

400g free range chicken – sliced

1/2 cup (127g) extra firm tofu

2 cloves garlic – minced

3 spring onions – sliced

1 free range egg

200g prawns

1 cup (80g) bean sprouts

2 tablespoons peanuts – crushed

lime wedges to serve

INSPIRATION

For a vegetarian option, leave out the chicken.

FISH TACOS

serves 4

Ingredients – Fish Marinade

4 white fish fillets – chopped into pieces
1 french shallot – finely diced
2 tablespoons lemon juice
1 tablespoon fresh coriander – finely chopped
2 tablespoons olive oil
pinch sea salt
1 clove garlic – minced
12 taco shells

Ingredients – Baja Sauce

1 cup df mayonnaise
2 avocados – peeled and pitted
6 jalapenos – seeded and chopped
3 tablespoons lime juice

Ingredients – Salsa Topping

1 ripe mango – peeled, pitted and diced
1 small cucumber – peeled and diced
2 tomatoes – diced
1/2 cabbage – finely shredded
4 sprigs coriander – finely chopped

Method

Combine all marinade ingredients in a bowl, cover and marinate fish fillets for 20 minutes in the fridge.

Place fish and marinade in a frying pan on medium heat.

Gently cook until fish is tender and put in a serving bowl.

Place Baja Sauce ingredients in a blender or food processor and blend until smooth. Place in a serving bowl.

Combine all salsa ingredients in a bowl.

Place taco shells on a baking tray and warm under the grill for 5 minutes.

Place all ingredients on the table for people to assemble their tacos as they feel.

RED FISH CURRY

serves 4

Ingredients

500g firm white fish fillets or
free range chicken – diced

375ml tin coconut milk

2 tablespoons gf fish sauce

1-2 tablespoons red curry paste

any vegetables – beans, baby eggplant,
pumpkin or zucchini – sliced

1 handful fresh coriander – chopped

Method

Pre-heat oven to 180C.

*In a 1.5l baking dish, place diced fish
or chicken.*

*In a jug, mix the coconut milk, fish sauce
and red curry paste.*

*Add vegetables to the baking dish and pour
the coconut milk mixture over the top.*

*Bake in the oven for 20-25 minutes
(UNCOVERED).*

Stir in coriander and serve.

CHICKEN CURRY WITH CARDAMOM & STAR ANISE

serves 4

Ingredients

1 tablespoon mild curry powder or massaman curry paste

1 brown onion – diced

1 tablespoon peanut oil

1 1/2 star anise

4 cardamom pods

500g free range chicken thighs, skinless and boneless – chop into small pieces

2 tablespoons gf fish sauce

2 tablespoons tamarind pulp

360ml coconut milk or water

6 prunes

fresh coriander to serve

sea salt to season

Method

In a heavy based saucepan, heat the peanut oil and add the onion, cooking it gently until translucent.

Add curry powder and sauté for 5 minutes.

Add coconut milk, star anise and cardamom pods.

Bring to a simmer.

Add chicken pieces and prunes and simmer for 10 minutes.

Add fish sauce and tamarind pulp and taste for salt.

Cover and continue to simmer for about 60 minutes.

Serve with fresh coriander.

LAMB & PUMPKIN CURRY

serves 4

Ingredients

500g lamb – diced

2 tablespoons garam masala

2-3 tablespoons vegetable oil

2 onions – thinly sliced

2 garlic cloves – thinly sliced

1 cup (200g) pumpkin – diced

1/2 cup (100g) red lentils

2 1/4 cups (600ml) hot vegetable stock (see page 135) or water

1 tablespoon curry paste

1 tablespoon tamarind paste

sea salt

2 tablespoons fresh mint or coriander – chopped

juice of 1 lemon

Method

Place lamb in a bowl and add garam masala, stir through until lamb is coated.

Allow to stand for 30 minutes.

In a large saucepan, add oil and brown lamb.

Transfer to a plate and set aside.

Add more oil to the pan and cook onions, garlic and pumpkin for 5 minutes until just cooked.

Add lentils, vegetable stock or or water, curry and tamarind pastes and return lamb to the saucepan.

Bring to the boil and simmer 25-30 minutes, stirring occasionally.

Curry will thicken.

Stir in mint or coriander and lemon juice.

Add sea salt to taste.

INSPIRATION

This recipe also works really well with a firm white fish.

MILD CHICKEN & SPINACH CURRY

serves 6

Ingredients

1 brown onion – peeled and chopped

1/2 cup (105g) red lentils

2 tablespoons mild curry powder

2 teaspoons ground coriander

1 teaspoon cumin seeds

1 sprig curry leaves

2 cups (500ml) water

8 free range chicken thighs, skinless – chopped into small pieces

225g fresh english spinach – chopped finely or frozen spinach – thawed and drained

1 tablespoon fresh coriander – chopped

salt and pepper

Method

Place onion and oil in a large heavy based saucepan and cook gently until translucent.

Add curry powder, spices and curry leaves, cook for 5 minutes.

Add red lentils and water, bring to the boil, cover and simmer gently for 10 minutes.

Add chicken and spinach.

Replace lid and simmer for a further 40 minutes or until chicken is cooked through.

Stir in fresh coriander and season to taste.

SAYUR LODAY (INDONESIAN VEGETABLE DISH)

serves 8

Ingredients

2 large firm tofu cakes – diced

1 medium onion – diced

5 spring onions – diced

5 candle nuts* – chopped

2 cloves garlic – minced

1 tablespoon shrimp paste*

1/4 cup (25g) dried prawns*

1/4 cup (25g) whitebait*

80g cabbage – sliced

160g french beans – chopped in half

8 baby corn – sliced lengthways

4 baby zucchini – sliced lengthways

160g carrots – sliced lengthways

300g fresh prawns

540ml tinned coconut milk

1/4 teaspoon turmeric powder

1 litre boiling water

gf glass noodles

oil

sea salt

*available from asian grocery stores

Method

Prepare carrot, zucchini, corn, beans and cabbage and put aside.

In a large saucepan, heat oil and add tofu pieces stirring consistently so they do not stick. Remove from the pan and put aside.

In a blender, combine onion, spring onion, candle nuts, garlic, shrimp paste and drained dried prawns and whitebait (chillies optional). Blend briefly into a paste (called rempah).

In a large saucepan, stir fry the rempah over a low heat.

Turn heat to high, add fresh prawns and about 1/4 cup coconut milk and simmer for about 5 minutes.

Add remaining coconut milk and bring to the boil. Add the vegetables, bring back to the boil and add the tofu. Add 1 litre of boiling water. Continue stirring for another 5 minutes until vegetables are just cooked.
Add the turmeric and sea salt to taste.

Place glass noodles in a bowl, cover with boiling water, leave for 5 minutes, drain and add to the soup.

EGG, TOFU & CHICKPEA CURRY

serves 6

Ingredients

4 tablespoons oil

2 onions – diced

1 teaspoon mustard seeds

1 stalk fresh curry leaves – washed and chopped

3 cloves garlic – crushed

1 teaspoon fresh ginger – grated

3-4 tablespoons curry powder

500ml hot water

1 cup either pumpkin/sweet potato/cauliflower or a bit of each – peeled and cubed

400g drained chickpeas – freshly cooked or tinned

270ml tin coconut milk

6 free range eggs – hard boiled

sea salt to taste

Method

In a large saucepan, heat the oil.

When hot, add mustard seeds and chopped curry leaves.

When seeds start popping, add chopped onions, garlic and ginger.

Fry until the onions are softened and slightly browned.

Add 1/2 cup hot water and curry powder to the saucepan and stir into a paste.

Fry on a low heat for about 1/2 hour.

Add your choice of vegetables and 1 to 1 1/2 cups hot water.

Add coconut milk.

When the pumpkin or the other vegetables are cooked, add the drained chickpeas and hard boiled eggs.

If mixture is too thick, add extra hot water or coconut milk.

Add sea salt to taste.

NOTES

~ Accompaniments ~

Bean & Garlic Mash | Quinoa raw and cooked | Crunchy Garlic Brown Rice, Sweet Potato Hash Browns | Vegetable Slice

CRUNCHY GARLIC BROWN RICE

Ingredients

2 cups brown rice

3 cups water

3 tablespoons olive oil

3 cloves garlic – minced

sea salt

Method

Cook rice as usual in a rice cooker.

Place 3 tablespoons of olive oil, garlic cloves and salt in the mortar and pestle or blender and thoroughly infuse.

Put 1 teaspoon of oil into a heavy based saucepan, add rice and pour the oil and garlic mix over the rice BUT DO NOT STIR.

Let cook without stirring for 15-20 minutes until bottom layer is brown and crunchy.

Turn upside down onto a plate and serve as an accompaniment to a meal.

LEMON & THYME QUINOA

serves 6

Ingredients

1 cup (185g) red quinoa

2 cups (250ml) water

1/2 lemon – juiced

2 tablespoons olive oil

sea salt and pepper to taste

1 shallot – diced

1 sprig fresh thyme

Method

Fry shallot in oil until translucent.

Place red quinoa in a saucepan.

Add lemon juice, shallots, salt, pepper and thyme and stir through.

Add 2 1/2 cups boiling water and simmer on the stove until liquid is absorbed.

CAULIFLOWER MASH

serves 6

Ingredients

1 cauliflower

1/4 cup (65ml) df, gf milk

1 tablespoon df margarine

Method

Cut cauliflower into florets of about equal size.

Steam cauliflower in a saucepan until very soft.

Remove and place in a bowl and mash as you would potatoes.

Add milk and margarine and fluff mixture up with a fork.

BRAISED CABBAGE

serves 4

Ingredients

1 shallot – finely chopped

3 cloves garlic – finely chopped

1/2 leek – thinly sliced

1/2 cup either savoy/chinese/red/green cabbage or a bit of each – roughly chopped

1/4 cup chicken stock (see page 134)

3 tablespoons extra virgin olive oil

salt

pepper

chilli (optional}

Method

Pour 3 tablespoons olive oil into a frying pan over a medium high heat.

Add the leek, shallot and the garlic and sauté until translucent.

Add the cabbage. You want some small and large bits of cabbage as it adds to the texture of the dish.

Turn the heat down to a medium heat and keep pushing the ingredients around to wilt the cabbage.

Add salt and pepper and the chilli.

Check that the ingredients are not becoming too dry and add a splash of olive oil if required.

As the dish starts to cook down, add the chicken stock.

Allow the dish time to slowly develop in the pan. This usually takes around 35 minutes.

INSPIRATION

Omit the leek and chicken stock.

Add the following ingredients where you would add the chicken stock:

2 tablespoons tomato paste, 1/2 teaspoon turmeric, 2 tablespoons lemon juice, and as a further option a small diced portion gf bacon or gf pork sausage.
Cook over a very gentle heat for 45 minutes to an 1 hour.

COOKING DRIED CHICKPEAS

serves 6

Ingredients

500g dried chickpeas

2 sprigs thyme

3-5cm piece kombu (sea vegetable)

1 bay leaf

1 clove garlic

pinch sea salt

Method

Place chickpeas in water so that they are completely covered, soak for 8-24 hours.

Discard soaking water and rinse.

Season with thyme, clove of garlic, bay leaf and sea vegetable.

Cook in lots of water, in a heavy based pan, for approximately 2 hours.

ONLY ADD SALT AT THE END OF COOKING or you will toughen the chickpeas.

Chickpeas are cooked when you can squash them with gentle pressure and there are no hard bits in the centre.

Once cooked you can freeze them until needed.

INSPIRATION

Soaked chickpeas can be easily stored in the freezer.

Divide soaked chickpeas into convenient portions covered with water and place in the freezer.

Simply defrost by simmering with the seasoning in a saucepan.

BEAN & GARLIC MASH

serves 4

Ingredients

3 cloves garlic – crushed

425g can cannellini or borlotti beans

olive oil

Method

Fry crushed garlic in olive oil until brown.

Add cannellini or borlotti beans, heat through.

Add a dash of olive oil and mash up.

Serve as a side dish.

SWEET POTATO HASH BROWNS

serves 4

Ingredients

1kg sweet potatoes – peeled and grated

1 onion – grated

1/2 cup (55g) chickpea flour

1 free range egg – lightly beaten

1/2 cup (125ml) df, gf milk

sea salt

olive oil for frying

Method

Combine all ingredients in a bowl.

Cover the bottom of a heavy based frying pan with 1cm olive oil.

Shape mixture into small fritters and cook until golden brown, approximately 2 minutes on each side.

VEGETABLE SLICE

serves 6 - 8 or makes 9 muffins

Ingredients

1/2 cup (125ml) df margarine – melted and cooled

1 onion – peeled and grated

1 1/2 cups (285g) sweet potato – peeled and grated

1 cup carrots (230g) – peeled and grated

1 cup zucchini (230g) – peeled and grated

1 cup (125g) gf breadcrumbs or chickpea flour

1 teaspoon gf baking soda

2 teaspoons sea salt

Method

Pre-heat oven to 160C.

Lightly grease a small baking tin or muffin tray.

In a medium bowl, thoroughly mix together all of the ingredients.

Spoon mixture into a tin, cover with a layer of baking paper and then with foil.

Bake in oven, remove the baking paper and foil after 30 minutes and continue baking for another 15 minutes until firm and golden brown.

Alternatively, pour mixture into a muffin tray and bake for 20-25 minutes.

~ Stocks, Sauces & Dressings ~

Berry Sauce | Chicken Stock | Citrus Salad Dressing | Garlic Sauce

CHICKEN STOCK

makes approximately 4 litres

Ingredients

2 free range chicken carcasses or free range chicken wings and thighs (total of 12)

2 carrots – chopped roughly with skin on

1 large onion – chopped roughly (skin on is fine)

1 leek – washed and chopped

2-3 celery sticks – chopped roughly

12 black peppercorns

1 bulb garlic – horizontally chopped in half

2 bay leaves

12 or so parsley stalks

2 well ripened tomatoes – chopped horizontally (for a darker stock)

3 stalks thyme

5 litres water

Method

Roast off chicken carcasses or pieces in the oven at 180C for 1 hour.

The wings and thighs may take longer, roast until golden brown.

Remove chicken from the oven and place in the bottom of a stock pot with all the ingredients added gently.

Top with 5 litres of water.

Bring to the boil over a high heat.

Once boiled, skim off any fat and foam.

Turn down to a gentle simmer, and cook for 6 to 8 hours.

Remove stock pot from the stove, cool slightly before straining the liquid into another pot, let cool to room temperature.

Use in soups, in stir fries or when cooking vegetables or freeze in portions for later use.

INSPIRATION

Serves 4: Ladle 4 cups of chicken stock into a saucepan. Add 1 chopped chilli, a 5cm piece of crushed lemongrass and a handful of coriander. Bring to the boil. Place cooked cold chunks of free range chicken in serving bowls and ladle 1 cup each of chicken stock over the top. Serve with freshly chopped spring onion.

VEGETABLE STOCK

makes approximately 1.5 litres

Ingredients

2 carrots – roughly chopped

1 leek – roughly chopped

1 large onion – roughly chopped with skin on

2-3 celery sticks – chopped

1 handful english spinach leaves

6 black peppercorns

2 well ripened tomatoes – halved horizontally

6 parsley stalks

3-4 thyme stalks

2 bay leaves

1 handful watercress

1 head garlic – halved horizontally

2 litres water

Method

Place all ingredients in a stock pot and cover with 2 litres water.

Bring to the boil.

Turn down the heat and allow to simmer for about 1 1/2 hours.

Allow to slightly cool and strain off liquid.

INSPIRATION

Pour stock into an ice cube tray and freeze. Once frozen, place stock cubes in a freezer bag for a quick and easy addition to all kinds of dishes.

WHITE SAUCE

Ingredients

1/3 cup (50g) gf flour

1/3 cup (50g) df margarine

300-350ml df, gf milk – warmed

pepper and sea salt

1/2 cup fresh parsley

Method

In a saucepan, melt the margarine and stir in the flour to form a roux.

Allow this mixture to cool.

Return to heat and gradually add the warmed milk, stirring all the time.

Simmer for approximately 2-3 minutes.

If the sauce is too thick, add a little more milk.

Add the parsley, pepper and sea salt.

FLOURLESS WHITE SAUCE

Ingredients

300g packet silken tofu

130g packet pine nuts

1 bunch chives

1 pinch sea salt

3 tablespoons lemon juice

Method

Add all ingredients to blender or food processor and mix until smooth.

HOLLANDAISE SAUCE

serves 4

Ingredients

3 tablespoons lemon juice

3 tablespoons water

1/2 teaspoon sea salt

3 free range eggs (1 egg plus 2 yolks)

200g df margarine

Method

Melt margarine in a small saucepan.

In another saucepan, combine the lemon juice and water, bring to a simmer and add the sea salt.

Crack 1 whole egg and the 2 yolks into a third small saucepan.

Vigorously beat the egg and yolks until pale and thick.

Set the yolk mixture over low heat and SLOWLY whisk in the hot lemon juice.

Continue whisking until you have a foamy warm mixture.

Remove from heat – DO NOT overheat.

Immediately start beating in the warm margarine, adding it SLOWLY.

You should have a thick, creamy and light sauce.

Add sea salt and pepper and more lemon juice to taste.

GARLIC SAUCE

(REALLY STRONG)

Ingredients

1 whole garlic

1/4 cup (60ml) oil
(canola makes a white coloured sauce)

1/4 teaspoon sea salt

1 tablespoon lemon juice

Method

Mince garlic cloves and scrape into the mortar and pestle.

Mix with salt until a paste is formed.

Spoon garlic and salt paste into a food processor.

*With the machine on, **add 1 teaspoon of oil at a time** until all the oil is used or the sauce stops thickening.*

Sauce will thicken to a mayonnaise-like consistency.

Add lemon juice while the blender is on.

INSPIRATION

Use as accompaniment to chicken and lamb or use during cooking to coat roast chicken and meat.

Keeps for 3-4 weeks in an airtight container in the fridge.

AIOLI WITH WASABI

makes approximately 200ml

Ingredients

2 free range egg yolks

2 tablespoons lemon juice

1 tablespoon gf, df wasabi

1 clove garlic – crushed

1/2 cup (125ml) vegetable oil

1 tablespoon hot water (optional)

1 pinch sea salt

Method

The type of oil you use in this recipe really impacts on the final flavour, so make sure your oil is not rancid.

Blend egg yolks, lemon juice and crushed garlic until smooth, adding small amounts of wasabi carefully as its flavour intensifies over time.

With your blender on, add oil GRADUALLY in a thin stream and process until mixture thickens.

Thin aioli with hot water, if desired.

This will keep covered in the fridge for 3-4 days.

INSPIRATION

For a homemade mayonnaise, omit the wasabi and garlic.

For a flavoured mayonnaise, add fresh herbs.

CITRUS SALAD DRESSING

Ingredients

1 lemon – juiced

1 orange – juiced

1 garlic clove – crushed

1/2 teaspoon ginger – freshly grated

2 tablespoons oil

1 tablespoon wf tamari

Method

In a small bowl, mix all ingredients together.

This dressing is lovely served over a green salad.

SWEET ASIAN DRESSING

Ingredients

2 tablespoons coconut milk

1/2 tablespoon raw unprocessed honey

1/2 tablespoon sesame oil

Method

In a small bowl, mix all ingredients together.

BERRY SAUCE

Ingredients

350g fresh or frozen ripe strawberries
or raspberries

2 teaspoons strained lemon juice

1 tablespoon raw unprocessed honey

Method

Place all ingredients in a blender and process until smooth.

Press sauce through a sieve to remove seeds.

INSPIRATION

You can add a few drops of rose flower or orange blossom water to infuse the sauce with a different flavour.

~ Biscuits & Muffins ~

Honey Joys | Almond Crescents | Flourless Fruit Muffins

ALMOND CRESCENTS

makes 12

Ingredients

3 cups (330g) almond meal

3 free range egg whites

4 tablespoons raw unprocessed honey

3 drops vanilla extract (optional)

1 cup (80g) flaked almonds

Method

Pre-heat oven to 150C.

Combine almond meal, honey and vanilla essence in a large bowl.

Add egg whites and stir until mixture forms a firm paste.

Roll level tablespoons of the mixture into 8 cm logs, shape to form crescents and GENTLY roll in the flaked almonds.

Place on oven trays lined with baking paper.

Bake in the oven for about 15 minutes or until browned lightly.

Cool on trays.

INSPIRATION

Add the zest of 1 orange to the above recipe.

Add the zest of 1 lemon to the above recipe and replace the flaked almonds with shredded coconut for the coating.

COCONUT MACAROONS

makes 24

Ingredients

3 free range egg whites
(at room temperature)

1 1/2 cups (125g) ground almonds (optional)

1/4 teaspoon vanilla extract

1 1/2 cups (125g) desiccated coconut

2 tablespoons raw unprocessed honey

1/2 teaspoon cinnamon (optional)

Method

Pre-heat oven to 150C.

In a medium mixing bowl, whisk the egg whites and vanilla until stiff, glossy peaks are formed.

Gently fold in the honey.

Gently mix in the coconut, ground almonds and cinnamon.

Using a teaspoon, divide the mixture into walnut size pieces.

Place on a baking tray lined with baking paper.

Bake for 25 minutes.

The biscuits should be changing colour on the outside but stay soft on the inside.

FLORENTINES

makes 30

Make the sweetened condensed milk IN ADVANCE for this recipe.

Ingredients – Sweetened Condensed Milk

1/3 cup boiling water

1 cup gf soymilk powder

1/6 cup agave syrup

4 tablespoons df margarine – melted

Ingredients – Florentines

1/2 cup sultanas

2 cups gf cornflakes

3/4 cup slivered almonds (or peanuts) – chopped coarsely

1/2 cup craisins (substitution for cherries as they can contain glucose from wheat)

2 tablespoons finely chopped glaced ginger (optional)

2/3 cup gf, df sweetened condensed milk

200g df dark chocolate

Method – Sweetened Condensed Milk

Makes 1 cup of sweetened condensed milk:

Melt margarine in the microwave, add all ingredients to the blender and mix until creamy and thick.

Store in fridge until ready to use.

Method – Florentines

Pre-heat oven to 190C.

Line oven trays with baking paper.

Combine sultanas, cornflakes, nuts, craisins, ginger and gf, df sweetened condensed milk in a large bowl.

Drop rounded teaspoons of the mixture about 2cm apart on lined oven trays.

Bake for 10 minutes (Florentines should be browned), cool on trays.

Break chocolate into pieces, place in a microwave bowl and melt for 1 MINUTE AT A TIME, keep checking and stir until done.

With a knife, spread base of each Florentine with chocolate and leave upside down till chocolate sets. (They are just as good without chocolate or you can try df white chocolate.)

Florentines can be stored in an airtight container for up to two weeks.

COCONUT & ORANGE COOKIES

makes 20

Ingredients

1 cup coconut flour

1/2 cup chickpea flour

1/2 teaspoon gf baking powder

pinch sea salt

2 free range eggs

1/4 cup raw unprocessed honey

1/2 teaspoon vanilla essence

1 teaspoon cinnamon

2 teaspoons orange peel

2 tablespoons orange juice

2/3 cup df margarine or coconut oil – melted

Method

Pre-heat oven to 180C.

Place baking paper onto a flat baking tray.

Place all dry ingredients in a medium bowl.

Make a well in the centre adding eggs, honey, peel and juice and combine until mixed.

Add warm melted margarine and mix thoroughly.

Roll mixture into balls and place on baking tray, squashing them down GENTLY.

Bake for 20 minutes.

Leave for 5 minutes before transferring onto a wire rack to cool.

HONEY JOYS

makes 30

Ingredients

4 cups (900g) gf cornflakes

1/4 cup (125g) linseeds

1/4 cup (125g) pumpkin seeds

1/4 cup (125g) sunflower seeds

1/3 cup (115g) raw unprocessed honey

90g df margarine

Method

Pre-heat oven to 180C.

Add all dry ingredients to a bowl.

*Gently melt margarine and honey,
DO NOT let boil.*

*Mix melted butter and honey with the dry
ingredients and mix gently but well.*

Place patty pans onto a baking tray.

Spoon mixture into patty pans.

Bake for 10 minutes – until golden.

*For crispier honey joys, allow to cool on the
baking tray.*

FLOURLESS FRUIT MUFFINS

makes 16 muffins

Ingredients

3 cups almond or any other nut meal

1/2 cup shredded coconut

1/2 cup oil

1/4 cup raw unprocessed honey

2 apples – finley diced

1/2 cup berries

2 free range eggs

1/2 cup (125ml) df, gf milk

Method

Prepare a 12 holed muffin tin with patty pans.

In a medium size mixing bowl, add all dry ingredients and the fruit.

Whisk together the egg, milk, honey and oil.

Add to dry ingredients.

Spoon ingredients into muffin tin and bake for 25 to 30 minutes at 180C.

TROPICAL MUFFINS

makes 12 muffins

Ingredients

1 cup (110g) gf plain flour

2 tablespoons raw unprocessed honey
or maple syrup

2 tablespoons gf baking powder

1 teaspoon cinnamon

2 free range eggs

1/2 cup (125ml) vegetable oil

1/2 cup (115g) carrots – finely grated

1/2 cup (115g) apples – finely diced

1/2 cup (115g) pineapple pieces – drained

1/2 cup (115g) moist coconut flakes

2 tablespoons orange zest – finely grated

1/4 cup (55g) macadamia nuts – chopped

Method

Pre-heat oven to 160C.

Prepare a 12 hole muffin tin with patty pans.

In a large bowl, mix together flour, baking powder and cinnamon.

In a medium bowl, beat eggs and oil together until blended.

Add the honey to the egg mixture.

Add the wet and dry ingredients and stir until just combined.

Add remaining ingredients and fold until combined.

Fill muffin cups 3/4 full.

Bake for 40 minutes or until muffins are golden brown and a skewer comes out clean.

Briefly cool in tin, turn out and place on a wire rack.

HONEY NUT CUPCAKES

makes 12

Ingredients

3/4 cup (175g) df margarine

1/3 cup (90g) raw unprocessed honey

3 free range eggs – beaten

3/4 cup (175g) gf flour

2 1/2 tablespoons gf baking powder

1 teaspoon xanthan gum (guar gum)

1/2 cup (115g) almond or hazelnut meal

1 teaspoon ground cinnamon

Method

Pre-heat oven to 180C.

Grease and place muffin cases in a 12 hole muffin tray.

In a large bowl, mix honey and margarine until light and creamy.

Mix in beaten eggs.

Mix in flour, baking powder, cinnamon and xanthan gum.

Stir in almond or hazelnut meal.

Divide mixture between muffin tins.

Bake for approximately 25 minutes until muffins are golden and skewer comes out clean.

Briefly cool in tin and place on wire rack.

VANILLA CUPCAKES

makes 12

Ingredients

225g df margarine

1/4 cup agave nectar

225g gf self-raising flour

1 teaspoon gf baking powder

4 free range eggs

1 teaspoon vanilla extract

Ingredients – Icing

140g df margarine

280g pure icing sugar

1-2 tablespoons df, gf milk

few drops vanilla extract

Method

Pre-heat oven to 175C.

Place all ingredients in a medium bowl and beat with electric beaters until smooth and pale.

Spoon mixture into 12 patty cases making them 1/2 to 3/4 full.

Bake for 20 minutes.

Cool in trays for 5 minutes before turning out onto cooling rack.

Decorate as desired.

Store in airtight container for 3 days or freeze for up to 3 months.

Method – Basic Icing

Beat the margarine in a large bowl until soft. Add half the icing sugar and beat until smooth.

Add the remaining icing sugar with one tablespoon of the milk and vanilla extract.

If required, add extra icing sugar to thicken or a little extra milk to make it thinner.

NOTES

~ Desserts ~

Very Lemony Tart | Almond & Coconut Cake | Non-Dairy Raspberry Cheesecake | Honey & Rose Pannacotta

FRUIT JUICE JELLY

serves 4

Ingredients

2 cups (500ml) unsweetened juice
(works well with apple and pear)

1 teaspoon agar agar

2 1/2 cups (450g) fresh fruit pieces

NOTE

1/2 teaspoon agar agar will set
1 cup of juice.

For highly acidic juices (pineapple,
orange,lemon), you will need to double the
amount of agar agar.

Method

Pour juice into a medium saucepan, sprinkle agar agar powder on top and whisk through.

Place saucepan on a gentle heat, bring the liquid to a gentle boil and continue for approximately 7 minutes stirring frequently to stop the agar agar from settling at the bottom.

Allow to cool for a few minutes.

Place fruit pieces into serving dishes and pour the juice and agar agar mixture over the top.

Allow to set for 1-2 hours.

GAAJAR KA HALWA (SWEET INDIAN PUDDING)

serves 8

Ingredients

4 cardamom pods

1 tablespoon df margarine

4 carrots – peeled and grated

1 cup (250ml) df, gf milk

2 tablespoons raw unprocessed honey

1/4 cup (35g) sultanas

8 each almonds, cashews, pistachios

Method

Crush cardamom pods in mortar and pestle and remove the husks.

Peel and grate carrots.

Melt margarine in a medium saucepan.

Add carrots and stir over medium heat for 6 minutes.

Add the milk and cook for 15 minutes, reducing the liquid and softening the carrots.

Add cardamom, honey, sultanas and nuts, cooking and stirring for another 30 minutes until liquid is reduced and you have soft carrots of a pudding-like consistency.

Check for sweetness and adjust if necessary.

Place in a serving bowl

Serve in small portions or cover and refrigerate, it keeps for 3 days.

CARROT & PECAN CAKE

serves 8

Ingredients

1 1/2 cups (340g) gf soy flour

1 teaspoon ground cinnamon

1/3 cup (85g) raw unprocessed honey

2 cups (500g) carrots – grated

1/2 cup (85g) dried apricots – finely chopped

1/2 cup (60g) pecans – chopped

1 cup (250ml) oil

4 free range eggs – lightly beaten

Method

Pre-heat oven to 160C.

Grease a 14cm x 21cm loaf tin and line with grease proof paper.

Sift flour and cinnamon into a large bowl.

Stir in honey, carrot, apricots and pecans.

Combine oil and eggs and stir into flour mixture.

Pour mixture into prepared loaf tin.

Leave in a moderately hot oven for 50 minutes or until firm.

Leave for 5 minutes before turning onto a wire rack to cool.

ALMOND & COCONUT CAKE

serves 8

Ingredients

1 1/2 cups (165g) ground almonds

3/4 cup (50g) desiccated coconut

1/4 teaspoon sea salt

1/3 cup (85g) agave syrup

4 free range eggs

1 1/2 teaspoons vanilla extract

1/4 teaspoon almond essence

200g df margarine

2 tablespoons flaked almonds

Method

Pre-heat oven to 160C and grease a 23cm shallow spring form.

Melt and cool margarine.

In a medium bowl, combine ground almonds, coconut and salt.

In a separate bowl, whisk together the eggs, vanilla, agave syrup and almond essence until mixed thoroughly.

Mix margarine into the egg mixture.

Pour the liquid mixture over the dry ingredients and stir together.

Pour into the cake tin and scatter the flaked almonds over the top.

Bake for 40 minutes or until it springs back when gently pressed.

Once cooled, remove from the tin and transfer to a wire rack.

APPLE CAKE

serves 8

Ingredients

185g df margarine

2 tablespoons raw unprocessed honey or pure maple syrup

2 free range eggs

1 cup (115g) gf self-raising flour

1-2 teaspoons gf baking powder

1 cup (110g) almond meal

df, gf milk

apples or try pears, plums or nectarines

cinnamon

Method

Pre-heat oven to 180C.

Prepare 24cm cake tin, grease the sides and line the base with baking paper.

In a medium sized bowl, mix together margarine and honey until light and creamy.

Add the eggs one at a time and beat the mixture.

Add remaining ingredients, except for the fruit and milk.

Mix together and add enough milk to make a sloppy batter.

Pour into a cake tin.

Slice up apples or other fruit and push into the top of the batter.

Sprinkle cinnamon over the top of the cake and fruit.

Bake for 35-40 minutes.

STICKY DATE PUDDING

serves 8

Ingredients

60g df margarine

2 tbsp agave syrup

250g fresh dates – pitted and chopped

1 cup (250ml) water

1/4 cup (125ml) pure maple syrup

1 teaspoon bicarbonate of soda

1 cup (130g) gf self-raising flour

2 free range eggs

1/2 teaspoon vanilla extract

Sauce Ingredients

1/4 cup (170g) brown sugar or raw unprocessed honey

2/3 cup gf soymilk

80g df margarine

1/2 teaspoon vanilla extract

1 tablespoon gf corn flour in 2 tablespoons cold water

THIS CAKE FREEZES REALLY WELL.

Method – Pudding

Mix the chopped dates, maple syrup and water together in a pan over medium heat.

Bring to the boil, reduce heat and cook for one minute until jam-like in consistency.

Remove from heat and stir in bicarbonate of soda, stand to cool.

Place margarine and add flour and agave syrup in a large mixing bowl and beat until light and fluffy.

Add eggs one at a time, beating well after each addition.

Add vanilla extract.

Fold the self-raising flour into the date mixture.

Pour into 20 cm square cake tin lined with baking paper or a 12 cup greased muffin tin for individual serves and bake at 190C for 30-40 minutes or until skewer comes out clean.

Method – Sauce

Combine all ingredients except corn flour in a saucepan. Bring to the boil. Add corn flour paste and whisk until thickened.

Reduce heat and simmer for 3 minutes.

Pour sauce over cut cake servings or individual sticky date puddings.

NON-DAIRY RASPBERRY CHEESECAKE

inspired by Jude Blereau

serves 6 - 8
The base and filling are best made THE DAY BEFORE and kept in the fridge overnight.

Ingredients – Base

(there is a biscuit base option under "Inspiration")

1 1/2 cups (150g) almond and hazelnut meal

1 cup (160g) sultanas

3 tablespoons almond or coconut oil

1/2 cup (63g) pecans

1/2 cup (48g) desiccated coconut

Ingredients – Filling

450g silken tofu

1 free range egg

3/4 cup (185ml) coconut milk

227g "tofutti cream cheese"
(optional, makes for a creamier texture)

40ml pure maple syrup

3 teaspoons natural vanilla extract

zest and juice of 1/2 lemon

1/2 cup (115g) raspberries (fresh or frozen)

Method – Base

Line 24 x 4cm ovenproof dish with baking paper.

Add all the base ingredients into a food processor and mix for 5 minutes until they stick together.

Press mixture into ovenproof dish, covering ONLY the base.

Method – Filling

Pre-heat oven to 120C.

Place all ingredients for the filling except raspberries in a food processor or blender and blend for 5 minutes until thick and smooth.

Add raspberries, blending for another 10 seconds.

Pour over the base and bake for 1 hour.

Allow to cool and place in the fridge overnight, then add the glaze the next day.

Ingredients – Berry Glaze

1/2 cup (125ml) water

1 3/4 cup (250g) raspberries or strawberries

1 tablespoon raw unprocessed honey

1/2 teaspoon agar agar

OPTIONAL – Crunchy Biscuit Base

180g gf plain sweet biscuits

1/2 cup (55g) almond meal

60g df margarine – melted

Place all ingredients in a food processor and mix until biscuits are crushed and the mixture is coming together.

Press into the base of a dish lined with baking paper and refrigerate until ready to use.

Glazing is optional ...

Method – Glazing

In a small saucepan, GENTLY boil berries and water for 8-10 minutes.

Press mixture through a sieve discarding the seeds.

Pour the liquid back into the saucepan, add honey and the agar agar powder stirring very gently, bring to the boil and simmer for 15-20 minutes.

Keep stirring so it does not stick to the bottom.

Let glaze cool, and then spoon over the cold cake.

INSPIRATION

If you find the filling not firm enough because the consistency of tofu varies, add 1/8 teaspoon of agar agar to a dash of boiling water, and stir into the filling.

PROFITEROLES

makes approximately 10 large profiteroles or 24 smaller ones

Ingredients

1/2 cup (125ml) water

1/4 cup (55g) df margarine

1/4 cup (40g) gf plain flour

1/4 cup (40g) fine white rice flour

2 free range eggs (59g each)

Method

Pre-heat oven to 220C.

Line an oven tray with baking paper.

In a small saucepan, add water and margarine and heat on high until boiling and margarine has melted.

Remove from heat, add flour all at once and beat vigorously with a wooden spoon until smooth and mixture comes away from the sides of the pan. It should look a bit gluey.

Method – CONTINUED

If the mixture does not come away from the sides, return saucepan to a very low heat for a few more seconds.

In a small bowl, beat the mixture using an electric mixer for 30 seconds.

Add eggs ONE AT A TIME beating well after each addition until dough becomes smooth and shiny.

Spoon walnut sized blobs onto a baking tray.

Bake for 20-25 minutes until the puffs have risen and are crisp and golden brown (try not to open oven door or they might collapse).

When the profiteroles are ready, remove them from the oven, transfer them to a wire rack and very quickly pierce them with a sharp knife around the middle; this allows the steam to escape and prevents them from going soggy.

INSPIRATION

Fill with fresh fruit and Vanilla Custard (recipe page 167).

Serve with df, gf vanilla ice cream and a fresh Berry Sauce (page 143).

VANILLA CUSTARD

serves 4

Ingredients

2 1/2 cups (625ml) df, gf milk

vanilla bean – split

6 free range egg yolks

2 tablespoons raw unprocessed honey
or pure maple syrup

a pinch of sea salt

Method

In a small saucepan, add milk and vanilla bean and simmer until just warm.

Leave in the saucepan for 10 minutes to infuse.

In a separate bowl, whisk together eggs and salt until frothy.

Pour in the warm milk and honey and whisk together.

Cook mixture over a low heat, stirring ALL THE TIME until the custard thickens.

Remove the vanilla bean, pour into a clean bowl and allow to cool.

Can be kept in the fridge for up to 3 days.

INSPIRATION

To make a thicker custard, add 2 tablespoons gf corn flour to 1/4 cup df, gf milk and whisk into the mixture.

STRAWBERRY ICE CREAM

serves 4

Ingredients

2 free range egg whites

1 cup castor sugar

2 punnets (500g) strawberries –
tops removed and cut into small bits

Method

Place all ingredients in a large mix master bowl.

Initially, beat on low speed until strawberries are mashed.

Then, beat on high speed until mixture becomes fluffy and rises to the top of the bowl.

Place mousse-like mixture into a glass bowl and freeze.

Can be enjoyed on its own or served with fruit salad.

INSPIRATION

Raspberry Ice Cream

500g raspberries, 1 teaspoon lemon juice, 1/2 cup castor sugar, 1 egg white

Whip all ingredients for 10 minutes using an electric beater.

Spoon into a container and place in the freezer until frozen.

APPLE & APRICOT COBBLER

serves 6

Ingredients

800g tin apples

410g tin apricots

1 banana – sliced

1/2 cup (115g) sultanas

1 teaspoon cinnamon

1/3 cup (85g) LSA
(linseed, sunflower and almond mix)

2 free range eggs

1/2 cup (115g) raw unprocessed honey

1 cup (125ml) oil

1 cup (110g) gf self-raising flour

Method

Pre-heat oven to 200C.

Place apples and apricots on the bottom of a greased pie dish.

Place chopped banana and sultanas on top of the apples and apricots and sprinkle with cinnamon and LSA.

Beat eggs and honey in a medium sized bowl until combined.

Add oil, mix well.

GRADUALLY add in the flour.

Spoon thick batter over apple mixture.

Bake for 45 minutes until golden brown.

HONEY & ROSE PANNACOTTA

serves 4

Ingredients

1 teaspoon gelatine
(or agar agar if you prefer)

2 tablespoons warm water

2 cups (500ml) gf soy or almond milk

2 1/2 tablespoons raw unprocessed honey

4 cardamom pods

1 splash rose water or rose syrup
concentrate

Method

Grind cardamom pods in the mortar and pestle.

*In a medium saucepan, add milk,
ground cardamom and honey.*

*Heat VERY GENTLY until just simmering and
honey is dissolved.*

*In a bowl, sprinkle gelatine over warm water
and stir until dissolved.*

*Whisk the dissolved gelatine through the milk
and honey mixture.*

*Add a splash of rose water or rose syrup
concentrate.*

*Place ramekin moulds on a flat tray lined with
a tea towel to catch any spills.*

*Pour mixture through a sieve into moulds,
discard any cardamom pieces, cover with
plastic and refrigerate for 3-4 hours.*

INSPIRATION

Serve with fresh strawberries and a drizzle of rose syrup. Or serve with chopped pistachios.

*For a more simple flavour, leave out the cardamom and use vanilla essence instead of rose water.
Or, for a very different flavour, use coconut milk and sweeten with orange juice.*

APPLE & RASPBERRY CRUMBLE

serves 6

Ingredients

4-6 large cooking apples

1/4 cup (75ml) pure maple syrup

1 cinnamon stick

1/4 cup (75ml) water

2 cups (275g) frozen raspberries
or blueberries

Ingredients – Crumble

4 tablespoons df margarine

4 tablespoons gf plain flour

4 tablespoons shredded coconut

4 tablespoons cashew nuts – roughly chopped

4 tablespoons LSA or gf muesli

4 tablespoons raw unprocessed honey

Method

Pre-heat oven to 180C.

Peel, core and cut apples into chunks.

Place in a saucepan with maple syrup, water and cinnamon stick.

Simmer gently until just soft and the pieces still hold their shape.

Pour into a baking dish, add berries and mix through.

Method – Crumble

Combine crumble ingredients by working margarine through with your hands.

Scatter over apples and berries.

Bake for 25 minutes or until crumble turns golden brown.

VERY LEMONY TART

1 large flan or 8 individual tarts

Ingredients – Shortcut Pastry

1 1/4 cups (200g) gf plain flour

2 tablespoons glutinous rice flour

3 tablespoons pure icing sugar (optional)

100g cold df margarine

1 free range egg

1 teaspoon lemon or lime juice

rind of 1 lemon – grated

Note

for a nutty pastry, add 1/4 cup hazelnut, almond or pecan meal

Method

Pre-heat oven to 180C.

Lightly grease a 24cm or 8 individual 8cm x 2cm loose bottomed flan tins.

Place flour and icing sugar in a bowl, add margarine and rub through mix till crumbly.

Whisk egg, lemon juice and rind together and add to dough mix.

Mix until dough comes together in a ball. If mixture is too wet, add more flour.

Roll out dough to the shape of the tin on a floured surface.

Transfer to the tin and press in with floured fingers.

Trim edges with a knife.

Place tin in the freezer for 15 minutes.

Bake for 20 minutes and allow to cool before filling.

CONTINUED ON NEXT PAGE ...

VERY LEMONY TART

... continued

Ingredients – Filling

zest of 3 lemons

3/4 cup (187ml) lemon juice

2 free range eggs + 2 yolks

1/4 cup (60ml) pure maple syrup

1 cup (100g) almond meal

100ml gf soy or almond milk or
df, gf cream substitute

Note

for a lighter filling, add an extra egg and omit
the almond meal.

Method

Pre-heat oven to 190C.

Place pre-baked flan shell onto a baking tray.

*Put the juice and finely grated lemon rind in a
large bowl.*

*Add the eggs, yolks, maple syrup, the almond
meal and the milk and whisk to combine.*

*Pour into pastry shell and bake for
20 minutes.*

FIG TART

serves 6

Ingredients – Filling

10 whole fresh figs

2 tablespoons raw unprocessed honey

Ingredients – Pastry

90g df margarine

1 cup (250ml) water

2/3 cup (150g) gf flour

2g xanthan gum

2 medium free range eggs

Method – Pastry

Pre-heat oven to 210C.

In a heavy based saucepan, combine the water, salt and margarine.

Bring to a simmer and add the flour and xanthan gum.

Lower temperature and continue cooking until pastry comes away from the sides and is well combined.

Method – CONTINUED

Remove from heat and cool to room temperature.

Whisk eggs and add SLOWLY to flour mix, combine thoroughly.

Knead pastry on a floured surface until shiny.

Wrap pastry in glad wrap and chill.

Remove the pastry from the fridge and roll it between two pieces of baking paper with a rolling pin.

Roll out into a flan dish.

Place in the oven and bake for 10 minutes.

While the pastry is cooking, gently cut a cross into the top of each fig and open just a little.

Remove pastry and arrange the figs on top. Return to oven and cook for 15 minutes. Drizzle with a little honey when it comes out of the oven.

LEMON POLENTA CAKE WITH LEMON ICING

Ingredients – Cake

130g ground almonds (or use almond meal)

130g shredded coconut

130g fine polenta

1 teaspoon gf baking powder

grated rind of 3 lemons

3 lemons – juiced

150g df margarine

170g coconut oil

1/4 cup agave nectar

4 free range eggs (55g each)

1 teaspoon vanilla essence

Ingredients – Lemon Icing

250g icing sugar

juice of half a lemon (approximately)

Method

Pre-heat oven to 160C.

Combine ground almonds, coconut, polenta and baking powder in a bowl.

Stir in the grated lemon rind.

In a separate bowl, beat coconut oil, margarine and agave nectar together until pale.

Add eggs ONE AT A TIME, beating well after each addition.

Beat in the vanilla.

Fold in combined dry ingredients.

Add lemon juice until just combined.

Line base of 24cm cake tin with baking paper, grease the sides of the tin and pour in mixture.

Bake for 1 hour or until golden and just coming away from the sides of the tin.

This cake can be very fragile, so allow it to cool properly before turning out of the tin.

Unglazed cake will keep refrigerated in an airtight container for up to 1 week.

This cake also cuts more easily if refrigerated.

INDEX

BREAKFAST   **19**

Classic Chopped Fruit & Nuts   20

Nut Cream   21

Rhubarb & Pear Compote   22

Breakfast Quinoa (with Apple & Blueberries)   23

Quinoa with Ginger & Orange (INSPIRATION)   23

Almond & Chickpea Breakfast Pancake   24

Chickpea Pancake with Hummus & Avocado (INSPIRATION)   24

Chickpea Pancake with Banana & Passionfruit (INSPIRATION)   24

Chickpea Pancake with Strawberries (INSPIRATION)   24

Chickpea Pancake with Fruit Spread (INSPIRATION)   24

Crepes   25

Banana & Egg Pancake   26

Fruit & Nut Loaf   27

Corn Fritters (with Salmon & Rocket)   28

Frittata with Tuna, Sprouts & Tomato   29

Frittata with Ham, English Spinach & Capsicum (INSPIRATION)   29

Homemade Baked Beans   30

Chicken Thighs with Homemade Baked Beans (INSPIRATION)   30

Persian Eggs   31

A Cooked Breakfast   32

Sausage Roast   33

Breakfast Smoothie   34

Chai Tea	35
SNACKS	**37**
Pumpkin & Tuna Sushi (Rice Free)	38 - 39
Crunchy Spiced Dhal	40
Spicy Lime Nuts	41
Tuna Stacks	42
Chicken Pakoda	43
Chicken Nuggets (INSPIRATION)	43
Cauliflower Pakodas (INSPIRATION)	43
Chicken Meatballs	44
Lamb Meatballs (INSPIRATION)	44
Open Kofta with Tzatziki	45
Salt & Pepper Squid	46
Chilli Squid (INSPIRATION)	46
Chickpea Wrap with Avocado & Bacon	47
Seaweed Nori Wrap (INSPIRATION)	47
Sausage Rolls	48 - 49
Vietnamese Spring Rolls	50 - 51
Fried Saigon Spring Rolls	52
Thai Fish Cakes	53
Apple Date Slice	54
Craisin & Blueberry Slice (INSPIRATION)	54

Fruit & Nut Balls	55
Almond, Coconut & Carob Balls	56
Chilled Carob & Nut Slice	57

DIPS 59

Carrot Dip	60
Classic Eggplant Dip	61
Hummus	62
Hummus, Coriander & Chilli Dip (INSPIRATION)	62
Hummus & Pumpkin Dip (INSPIRATION)	62
Felafel with Hummus & Salad (INSPIRATION)	62
Avocado Salsa	63
Beetroot Dip	64
Tuna & Canellini Dip	65
Dukkah	66
Pesto	67
Tofu, Spinach & Garlic Dip	68
Sambal	69

SALADS 71

Broccoli & Cashew Salad	72
Quinoa Tabbouleh	73
Simple Green Salad	74
Mango & Cabbage Salad	75
Asian Slaw	76

Zeleta (Middle Eastern Salad)	77
Roasted Corn Salad	78
Cauliflower Salad	79

SOUPS — 81

Vietnamese Pho Ga	82 - 83
Pumpkin Soup	84
Pumpkin Soup with Macadamia Nuts & Corn Kernels (INSPIRATION)	84
Fresh Tomato Soup	85
Vegetable Soup	86
Green Curry Chicken Chowder	87
Gazpacho (Spanish Cold Soup)	88
Celeriac & Spinach Soup	89
Chicken & Corn Soup	90

MAINS — 93

Gado Gado	94 - 95
Coconut Chicken & Asian Salad	96
Mixed Dhal	97
Pesto Chicken	98
Crumbed Fish	99
Polenta Coated Patties	100
Garlic Prawns	101
Roast Chicken	102 - 103
Chicken Schnitzel	104

Chilli Con Carne	105
Simple Mediterranean Chicken	106
Pork Stir Fry with Noodles	107
Pork & Cabbage Stir Fry (INSPIRATION)	107
Eleven Veg Shepherd's Pie	108
Seafood Stew	109
Pasta Free Chicken Lasagne	110 - 111
Eggplant Stew	112
Pad Thai	113
Fish Tacos	114
Red Fish Curry	115
Chicken Curry with Cardamom & Star Anise	116
Lamb & Pumpkin Curry	117
Mild Chicken & Spinach Curry	118
Sayur Loday (Indonesian Vegetable Dish)	119
Egg, Tofu & Chickpea Curry	120

ACCOMPANIMENTS 123

Crunchy Garlic Brown Rice	124
Lemon & Thyme Quinoa	125
Cauliflower Mash	126
Braised Cabbage	127
Cooking Dried Chickpeas	128
Bean & Garlic Mash	129
Sweet Potato Hash Browns	130

Vegetable Slice	131

STOCKS, SAUCES & DRESSINGS — 133

Chicken Stock	134
Chicken, Lemongrass & Coriander Soup (INSPIRATION)	134
Vegetable Stock	135
White Sauce	136
Flourless White Sauce	137
Hollandaise Sauce	138
Garlic Sauce	139
Aioli with Wasabi	140
Mayonnaise (INSPIRATION)	140
Citrus Salad Dressing	141
Sweet Asian Dressing	142
Berry Sauce	143

BISCUITS & MUFFINS — 145

Almond Crescents	146
Coconut Macaroons	147
Florentines	148
Coconut and Orange Cookies	149
Honey Joys	150
Flourless Fruit Muffins	151
Tropical Muffins	152
Honey Nut Cupcakes	153

Vanilla Cupcakes	154
Basic Icing (INSPIRATION)	154

DESSERTS 157

Fruit Juice Jelly	158
Gaajar Ka Halwa	159
Carrot & Pecan Cake	160
Almond & Coconut Cake	161
Apple Cake	162
Sticky Date Pudding	163
Non-Dairy Raspberry Cheesecake	164 - 165
Profiteroles	166
Vanilla Custard	167
Strawberry Ice Cream	168
Raspberry Ice Cream (INSPIRATION)	168
Apple & Apricot Cobbler	169
Honey & Rose Pannacotta	170
Apple & Raspberry Crumble	171
Very Lemony Tart	172 - 173
Fig Tart	174
Lemon Polenta Cake with Lemon Icing	175

Photographs

AUTHORS' NOTE

We are neither nutritionists or naturopaths, nor do we have a medical background, have coeliac disease or have been diagnosed with intolerance to certain foods. We are students of the ageless wisdom and the collaboration for this book has come together by the teachings brought through by Serge Benhayon, founder and director of Universal Medicine.

Nina Stabey is a nutritionist and naturopath and is also the founder of The Healing Ingredient. She shared with us her knowledge of wheat, gluten and dairy, and this assisted us to have more of an understanding of what these foods do to us in our bodies. This information has been shared with you in Bridging Foods.

Natalie Benhayon assisted with the editing and writing of our 'Introduction to Bridging Foods'. She shared her wisdom with us on Bridging Foods and developed us into the greater understanding of the true intention of this book. She got us to feel that Bridging Foods is not 'our book', but that it is us sharing with you the collaboration on recipes and information gathered over a period of time in and from our unfolding and lived experiences as initiated by the teachings of Universal Medicine.

Bridging Foods offers the opportunity to consider the possibility that eating healthy is important, but equally important is to discern what certain foods and dishes feel like in your body and develop an understanding of what your body shows you about the way you eat, and the knowing of what to eat that is true to you and your body.

NOTES